Living Through History

The 1960s

Elizabeth Campling

B.T. Batsford Ltd London

Frontispiece
A "love-in" in Hyde Park, August 1967 (*Popperfoto*).

Cover Illustrations
The colour photograph shows astronaut Aldrin posing for a photograph beside the American flag during the Apollo II mission, 1969 (*N.A.S.A.*); the black and white print on the left is of the Beatles in 1963/4 (*Camera Press/Philip Gotlop*); the right-hand print shows riot police in Paris, 1968 (*Camera Press/Bryn Campbell*).

Typeset by Tek-Art Ltd, West Wickham, Kent
Printed in Great Britain by
R J Acford
Chichester, Sussex
or the publishers
B.T. Batsford Ltd
4 Fitzhardinge Street
London W1H 0AH

ISBN 0 7134 5570 5

ACKNOWLEDGMENTS

The Author and Publishers would like to thank the following for their kind permission to reproduce illustrations: Associated Press for figures 9, 15, 48 and 53; Associated Press/Wide World for figures 7, 11, 12, 17, 18, 23, 42, and 58; BBC Hulton Picture Library (U.P.I./Bettmann Newsphotos) for figures 8, 51 and 54; Camera Press for figures 1, 2 (F.J. Wymer), 3 (P.R./L.A.T.), 4 (Christopher Angeloglou), 5 (Relang), 6 (Anthony Fisher), 10 (James Pickerell), 13, 16 (Colin Davey), 19 (Richard Harrington), 20 (Z/B), 21, 22 (Graham Keen/London Look), 24 (Ray Hamilton), 26 (Leon Herschtritt), 27 (Bryn Campbell), 28 (Ken Welsh), 30 (Philip Gotlop), 32 (Apple/M.Fresco), 33 (L. Porter), 34 (T.S./R.B.O.), 35 (N. Gutman), 36 (C.A.P.A.), 38 (David Robison), 39 (N.C.N.A.), 40 and 41 (Rory Dell), 43 (Brian Aris), 44 (C.T.K.), 45 (Jevan Bebrange/R.B.O.), 46 (Stefan Tyszko/Queen), 47 (E.R.M.A.), 55 (Peter Simins/Pix Inc.) and 59 (G/M); C.B.S. for figure 31; I.D.A.F. for figure 37; N.A.S.A. for figure 50; National Film Archive for figures 14 and 49; Popperfoto for figures 29, 52, 56, 57 and 60. The pictures were researched by David Pratt.

The Author and Publishers would also like to thank the following organizations for permission to reproduce copyright material: Westminster Music Limited, 19-20 Poland Street, London W1R 3DD for the extracts from "Satisfaction" (p. 36) by Mick Jagger and Keith Richard, © Westminster Music 1965, and "A Whiter Shade of Pale" (p. 37) by Keith Reid and Gary Brooker, © Westminster Music 1967 (International copyright secured. All rights reserved.); Warner Bros Music Limited for extracts from "The Times They Are 'A Changin'" (p. 37) by Bob Dylan, © M. Witman & Sons 1964; CBS Songs for extracts from "Strawberry Fields" (p. 38) by John Lennon and Paul McCartney, © Northern Songs under licence to SBK Songs. "San Francisco" by Scott MacKenzie (p. 37) is published by MCA Music.

CONTENTS

THE ILLUSTRATIONS

THE 1960s IN PERSPECTIVE

In the decade following the end of the Second World War, most adults in the Western world (this included Japan) had come to be, on the whole, satisfied with their lives. Many felt – I was among them – that once again man had survived an ordeal of tremendous dimensions, unimaginable before. In Germany, where total war had brought what seemed like nearly total annihilation, we went in droves to Thornton Wilder's play "The Skin of our Teeth", perhaps the most popular drama on the German stage, where the title had been rendered as "Wir sind einmal davongekommen" ("Once More we have Survived"). Peace reigned, apart from some local conflicts. . . . Prosperity had returned to the industrialised countries, surpassing anything before. (K. Meinert, *Twilight of Youth*, Stuttgart, 1976)

1 The modern city centre of Frankfurt-on-Main, West Germany. Out of the ruins of war a prosperous Europe was rebuilt.

2 Another facet of post-war affluence – the library at the new University of Sussex on the south coast of England. By 1960 far more young people had access to higher education than ever before.

This was one middle-aged German's impression of the years leading up to 1960. He was not alone, for optimism was in the air. For the first time in human history it seemed possible to build a world in which poverty, violence and war would be eradicated. It was of the boundless opportunities the future seemed to offer that President John F. Kennedy spoke in his Inaugural Speech on 20 January 1961, when he told his audience that "Man holds in his mortal hands the power to abolish all forms of human poverty and all forms of human life."

Extremist politics went out of fashion in the West. If society were affluent enough it should be possible to wipe out poverty through greater productivity and without taking away anything from those who already had enough. The differences between right- and left-wing political parties narrowed to small differences of emphasis. This was labelled "consensus politics". Even the colonial wars that haunted the European news bulletins of the 1950s seemed soluble after 1959, when the governments of Britain and France declared themselves in favour of a rapid transfer of power to democratically elected nationalist governments in Asia and Africa. There seemed no reason why the Third World should not settle down to reap the twin benefits of Western democracy and economic growth.

No one denied that serious problems remained, among them the ever-present danger of a nuclear confrontation between the superpowers, for by 1960 the world possessed between 10 and 20 times the nuclear capacity it needed to destroy itself. The United States watched with growing unease the escalating Communist insurgency in South Vietnam and

3 One of the 1960s "hot-spots". The Cuban leader, ▶ Fidel Castro, addresses a crowd in Havana on the tenth anniversary of Cuban independence, 1 January 1969.

the increasing radicalism of Castro's government in Cuba. On the fringe of world politics stood the People's Republic of China, potentially one of the most powerful countries on earth, virulently anti-Western and immersed in domestic, political and economic struggles few Westerners fully understood. In 1960, however, there was still confidence that Western money and dedication could win the battle for the hearts and minds of the Third World. Walt Rostow, Special Assistant to President Johnson of the United States, wrote in 1964, when the dream was about to be shattered:

What is common throughout these regions is that men and women are determined to bring to bear what modern science and technology can afford in order to elevate the standards of life of their peoples and provide a firm basis for positions of national dignity on the world scene.

The U.S. is firmly committed to support this effort.

Underneath the surface calm of Western societies, however, there were signs that all was not well. The opening of John Osborne's *Look Back in Anger* at the Royal Court Theatre in London in 1956 heralded a spate of novels and plays by the "Angry Young Men". What they felt about life in post-war Britain is expressed most graphically by Jimmy Porter, the main character in *Look Back in Anger*:

I suppose people of our generation aren't able to die for good causes any longer. We had all that done for us, in the thirties and forties, when we were still kids. There aren't any good, brave causes left. If the big bang does come, and we all get killed off, it won't be in aid of the old-fashioned grand design. It'll just be for the Brave New Nothing-very-much-thank-you. About as

pointless and inglorious as stepping in front of a bus.

In the United States Beat poets such as Allen Ginsburg wrote of their disillusion with affluent America and inspired the cult of the "beatnik", who opted out of conventional society for a footloose life. When governments failed to act, frustrated citizens began to take matters into their own hands. The American civil rights movement, which began with the Montgomery, Alabama, bus boycott of 1955, and the Campaign for Nuclear Disarmament in Britain, which was founded in 1958 and which in 1959 attracted 50,000 on its annual march to the nuclear weapons research establishment at Aldermaston, are examples of this.

The 1960s are still very close, and historians agree that it is far more difficult to interpret the recent past than to make sense of what

4 The philosopher and mathematician, Bertrand Russell, addressing a C.N.D. rally in Trafalgar Square.

happened long ago. It may well be that future historians will see things quite differently, playing down some aspects that seem important today and emphasizing others. From the vantage point of the Eighties, however, it is as if a number of developments that had been quietly brewing throughout the 1950s suddenly boiled over to create ten years of extraordinary energy and ferment.

The opening years of the decade were characterized by great government-sponsored schemes to spread the fruits of the affluent society more widely. The New Frontier and Great Society in the United States, the promises of the Labour government elected in

Britain in 1964, the early years of American involvement in Vietnam, the model democratic constitutions granted to the newly independent African and Asian states – all were born in a spirit of optimism and all foundered far short of their goals.

At the same time, a great burst of self-awareness erupted among Western youth. Accepted codes of dress and behaviour were abandoned in the search for something that belonged uniquely to the young. Fashions in dress, decor, art and music changed with astonishing rapidity. The new heroes and trend-setters were pop-stars and fashion-designers. Their opinions on everything from hairstyles to politics were taken seriously. Overnight, the face of many cities changed. Here is one man's description of "Swinging London" in the summer of 1965:

The transformation that had come over London by that summer was indeed remarkable. In the

◄ **5** The fashions of the 1960s broke through traditional barriers of colour and style. This French outfit featured a patterned gold and green coat and tights over a skimpy yellow dress.

6 Skirts went on getting shorter – the King's Road, Chelsea 1967.

streets, the eye was arrested by the strangely-garbed young men with shoulder-length hair, girls in skirts for the first time eye-catchingly shorter than even the shortest skirts worn in the 1920s and clad from head to toe in the violent colours of plastic PVC or the dazzling blacks and whites of Op-Art. Down Carnaby Street and the King's Road the first of a flood of foreign tourists had already been drawn to gaze in awe at this thing that had happened to old England – picking their bemused way past the little "boutiques" which were springing up almost day by day with names like "430" and "Avant Garde" and "Domino" and "Countdown". (C. Booker, *The Neophiliacs*, London, 1969)

Not only among the young was there a growing irreverence towards established institutions. In Britain, "That was the Week that Was", a satirical television programme poking fun at Establishment figures including cabinet ministers and the Royal Family, drew an audience of millions. Even the Roman Catholic Church was affected. In 1962 Pope John XXIII convened the Vatican II Council to bring the Church into line with the modern world. One of its earliest reforms was the introduction of the vernacular mass in 1964.

As the decade progressed, the complaints of a few young people that life in the affluent West was materially comfortable but spiritually barren grew into a flood, triggering off a mass search for an alternative and more meaningful life. Some took the hippie road, opting out of conventional society altogether. Others banded together to overthrow existing society and replace it with something new and better. The universities, in particular, became hot-beds of discontent.

It was in the spirit of the age that people no longer meekly accepted situations they found

8 During the course of a march through Mississippi ▶ in favour of voter registration, 68-year-old Tom Flowers signs the electoral register for the first time in his life.

unpleasant or unjust. The failure of the civil rights movement to improve the living standards of America's urban Blacks, the rising revulsion with the Vietnam War, an unpopular proposal to build a new airport near Tokyo – all brought people out on to the streets. Even behind the Iron Curtain, where Communist Party control seemed unshakable, the system was challenged by the "Prague Spring" of 1968.

All this can only be understood in the context of the confident and affluent world of 1960. Flamboyant fashions in dress and music, the leisure for soul-searching, even the time to demonstrate, were all only possible in societies whose people no longer had to wonder where the next meal was coming from. The spread of mass education, especially higher education, and the growing influence of the mass-media made many people more assertive and aware. The Vietnam War may well have been no more savage than many previous wars, but the television news brought the atrocities into every living room and no one could hide from what was going

7 The universities were at the centre of the youthful rebellion against society. Here students at Berkeley, California, hold a silent vigil for a man wounded in rioting a few days before. Facing them are armed National Guardsmen, who are wearing masks in case tear gas needs to be used to disperse the demonstrators.

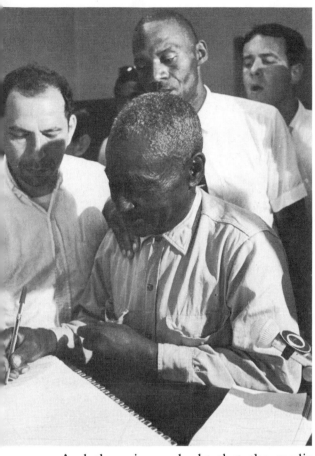

on. And there is no doubt that the media played an important role in the spread of fashions and ideas, both trivial and serious. The media created the pop cult, and Peter Smith, whose story appears on pages 17-20, is convinced that it helped to foster the

disaffection of the young, for so much attention was paid to every protest and demonstration that young people fell in love with their own image.

Decades seldom end on schedule and the 1960s was no exception. In 1970, for example, student unrest erupted once more at Nanterre in France, and state troopers shot four students during a protest rally against the Vietnam War at Kent State University in Ohio. The main wave of dissent, however, had passed its peak and did not recur. When the flood receded, much had changed. Throughout the West, societies would never be the same again, and the conventions, big and small, that the 1960s had torn down would not be resurrected. Gone too, however, was the optimism and confidence that had been the hallmark of 1960. In its place was a more cautious, more selfish and, some would say, more realistic mood. Perhaps the last word should rest with Jerry Rubin, a prominent American radical of the 1960s who in 1980 took a job with a public relations firm in New York. He told *The New York Times*:

Politics and Rebellion characterized the Sixties. The search for self characterized the spirit of the seventies. Money and financial interest will capture the passions of the Eighties. . . . If I am going to have any effect on my society in the next forty years, I must develop the power that only the control of money can bring. . . . Welcome, Wall Street, here I come!

A DECADE OF HOPE AND DISILLUSION

For better or for worse your generation has been appointed by history to deal with these problems and to lead America towards a new age. You have the chance never before afforded to people in any age. You can help build a society where the demands of morality and the needs of the spirit can be realized in the life of the nation.

So will you join in the battle to give every citizen full equality . . . whatever his belief, race or the colour of his skin? Will you join in the battle to give every citizen an escape from the crushing weight of poverty? (President Johnson announcing the Great Society campaign at the University of Michigan, Ann Arbor, 22 May 1964)

In the early 1960s it was easy to believe that prosperity and justice could be spread worldwide. By March 1963, 5000 young Americans, inspired by Kennedy's inaugural address, were serving abroad in the Peace Corps. In Britain, the Labour Party promised to modernize the country and to spread the benefits of modernization to *all* citizens. Future Prime Minister Wilson's glowing description of the "White Hot Technological Revolution" helped his party win the 1964 general election and end 13 years of Conservative government. In 1963 President Kennedy of the United States sent 10,000 American marines to the tiny country of South Vietnam to defend it against Communist insurgents, the Vietcong. Three years later there were over half a million American soldiers fighting there. Although the war later became very unpopular, many of the early conscripts went with a sense of mission, in the belief that they were defending freedom and democracy and had the support of the ordinary Vietnamese people. Many Africans believed that prosperity would follow hard on the heel of independence.

As early as 1965 the dream was turning sour. There was no one simple reason for this. Complex social problems proved far more difficult to solve than the optimists of 1960 had assumed. In the first place the idea that no problem was so big it could not be solved by generous funding proved illusory. American educationalists, for example, were shocked to discover that providing schools with more teachers and resources did not automatically improve the reading scores of black children. Human frailty played its part. Those who stood to lose most often obstructed reform, as civil rights campaigners in the southern United States discovered. Rightly or wrongly, many in Britain believed that Labour's economic reforms were undermined from the

9 Hopes of a democratic future for independent Africa were soon shattered. Four days after a military coup toppled the government of Kwama Nkrumah his headless statue lies in the grounds of the police headquarters in Accra.

start by the City of London and foreign bankers. Funds were diverted by corruption, a factor that was to play a large part in the downfall of Nkrumah, President of Ghana, the first black African state to become independent. The Vietnam War, which had once seemed a simple political issue, became a moral dilemma for many ordinary Americans when media coverage or personal involvement brought the reality of war into their own lives. Leslie Gelb, a Pentagon (War Office) official often returned home to his wife, who had been watching the news, to be asked: "What are you guys doing out there?" (Quoted in Luce and Sommer, *Vietnam: The Unheard Voices*, Cornell University Press, 1969)

Much *was* achieved in the 1960s, as is illustrated by the story of Wilma King Hunter on page 20, but many were disappointed. A backlash among those whose hopes had been awoken and then frustrated was all but inevitable. On 9 August 1965 rioting broke out in Watts, a black suburb of Los Angeles.

10 A political career in ruins. Shattered by his personal unpopularity at the height of the Vietnam War, President Johnson addresses the American people in April 1968 and announces that he has decided not to run for re-election in November.

11 Soldiers of the California National Guard patrol the streets of Watts, Los Angeles, after three days of violent rioting.

Over the next few years the same happened in other American cities including Detroit, and Washington. Lou Smith, a community worker, explained something of what was going through the rioters' minds:

There wasn't a damn soul paying one bit of attention to what was going on in Watts, so the black people in Watts just spontaneously rose up one day and said: "F _ _ _ it! We're hungry. Our schools stink. We're getting the s _ _ _ beat out of us. We've tried the integration route. It's obvious the integration route ain't going to work. Now we've got to go another way." (Quoted in G. Hodgson, *America in Our Time*, New York, 1978)

Many young Blacks rejected the peaceful methods of Martin Luther King in favour of Black Power, for, in the words of Stokeley Carmichael, "This country don't run on love, Brothers, it runs on power and we ain't got none." The Roman Catholic minority in Northern Ireland, long treated as second-class citizens, took to the streets in 1968 to demand civil rights and precipitated a crisis that persists today. In Africa "model" democracies collapsed under the weight of frustrated expectations. By 1969 Ghana, Zambia, Kenya, Uganda and Malawi had all abandoned democracy for dictatorship or military rule, and Nigeria had been plunged into civil war.

David Parks, an American in Vietnam

David Parks was born into a middle-class black family in the northern United States. As a boy he was comparatively sheltered from the poverty and racial prejudice endured by many black Americans, and by the age of 21, when he was drafted into the army, he was a light-hearted, politically uncommitted young man. At his father's suggestion, he kept a diary recording his experiences between his call-up for basic training in November 1965 and his final discharge in September 1967. This diary was published as *G.I. Diary* in New York in 1968.

Parks was a reluctant soldier, but only because army life promised to be dangerous and uncomfortable. He did not disagree in principle with the war and never dreamed of evading call-up, as many of his contemporaries had done. At training camp, however, he encountered marked racial prejudice for the first time and doubts arose in his mind about America's self-proclaimed mission as the defender of freedom in Vietnam:

This white sergeant, Morris, is the one who is pouring it on. Doesn't like the way I dress, stand, walk or talk. He stays on my back. . . . Never had such bad feelings against white guys before. . . . They don't let you forget you're colored or that they're white for one minute. . . . It's stranger still when you think that we are all going supposedly for the same cause – when half of us don't have a decent word for the other half. When we stand out there and salute the flag or march down the road to cadences, we're together. Other times – forget it. I can't imagine some of the southern cats liking me any better than they'll like the Vietcong. They'll probably treat the Vietnamese civilians like they treated the black people back where they came from. It makes you wonder about what is happening over there.

12 Black and white fought together in Vietnam, but ▶ racial tensions often ran high.

This feeling intensified when he and a friend left the base for an evening in the local town:

We went into a lily-white restaurant and ordered a pizza. We finally got it after waiting half an hour and it was partially raw. We tasted it, flipped our money down and walked out without eating it. The waiter laughed when we left. Hell, to think that both of us might die for a country where you can still be treated like that.

Private Parks arrived in Vietnam on active service on 1 January 1967 and joined a tank company in the Mekong Delta region.

Fighting a war against guerillas who sheltered among the local population was a nerve-wracking ordeal for young, inexperienced soldiers, for every village they entered might be death-trap. Decent men became trigger-happy and lost their humanity. David Parks himself was not immune. Six months after the start of his combat duty he wrote in his diary:

I think I'm getting a little too casual about death. This morning we were out on patrol with an ARVN [South Vietnamese] unit when we spotted a guy about forty years old. He was sitting inside the tree-line. The ARVN sergeant suspected he

13 Homes destroyed by American aircraft in Vietnam. Under the pressures of war decent men often behaved inhumanely.

was a VC [Vietcong] and he tried to question him, but the guy tried to get away. The ARVN just gunned him down with his carbine. I don't even remember that he told him to halt. . . . When, after a few minutes, I found myself eating a can of C rations, I began to wonder about myself. But I finished it.

Seeing the damage done to civilians, he questioned the morality of the war:

I hate being in this place, but there is a job to be done. It's our job, so they tell us, but I don't know the whole story – and nobody seems to be explaining it to us, at least so it makes sense. I sometimes wonder if we are helping or hurting these poor people. If you've never seen poverty, come to Vietnam.

Discrimination against non-white soldiers was often blatant. Only a month after he arrived in Vietnam Parks wrote:

The FO's (Forward Operator's) job is one of the hairiest in a mortar platoon. He's on more patrols because an FO is required to be with the patrolling squad at all times, and there are only three FOs to cover sixteen squads. The odds are against him. Sgt Paulson hand-picks the men for this job. So far he's fingered only Negroes and Puerto Ricans. I think he's trying to tell us something.

Personal grievances led him to question the entire American system. On 11 August 1967 he recorded:

Read about the riots back in the States in some clipping she [Deidre, a girl friend] sent me. They have me confused, the police brutality and all. It makes me wonder whether we're fighting the right war.

Earlier, in April of that year, Parks had discovered that any soldier who gained a place at a college automatically became eligible for discharge. Using his father's influence, he won a place at Rochester Institute of Technology in New York State and left the army in September 1967. On the flight home he thought about all he had experienced since his call-up:

Looking down over the rice paddies I knew so well made me wonder if I had any right to be there. When I came into the army I had no questions but I am leaving with some. Back in basic they told us over and over again that these people needed help, that they were poor and didn't know how to solve their own problems. Well, there were times when we seemed to be doing them more harm than good.

There were other soldiers, black and white, who came back in the same mood and helped to create the anti-war deluge of the late 1960s. As a black soldier, however, David Parks had even more scores to settle with American society. He concluded his diary:

September 12, 1967, 4.20 p.m.
Just spotted the California coastline. Just 48 hours and I'll be out of this man's army. Homeward bound. Went across on the 13th and going home on the 13th. Must be my lucky number. The white guy who sold me my ticket at the airport gave me some really dirty looks. He pitched my ticket at me like I was dirt. There is nothing like the army to make you conscious of these things. . . . Well, I'm a Negro and I'm back home where color makes the difference.

Peter Smith, an English Rebel

1960 found Peter Smith studying for his "A" levels in the Sixth Form of a minor public school in Croydon, South London. He was (according to his own estimation) "just an ordinary, dutiful pupil, totally uncritical and unthinking, interested in sport but not at all interested in anything cultural or political". In the course of the next two years, however, all this was to change:

Round about 1960 there really did seem to be a new wind blowing, at least in the world outside school. Cinema was very important – all those films rediscovering northern working-class life, like *Room at the Top*, *A Taste of Honey* and *Saturday Night and Sunday Morning*. Theatres,

14 A still from *Saturday Night and Sunday Morning*, starring Albert Finney, one of the wave of British "realistic" films about working-class life.

too, were still putting on plays by the Angry Young Men – John Osborne and Arnold Wesker were still very popular. All this contrasted with the traditional stuff still being pumped out at school.

And the theatre and cinema were incredibly cheap. I could manage it on just an ordinary boy's pocket money. And there was a new mobility. This was the time when motor bikes became freely available and you could travel round quite cheaply. You weren't just trapped in your own area. And, for me, living near London was important; it exerted quite a pull.

Traditional school discipline, with its emphasis on unquestioning obedience, suddenly seemed intolerable. So, too, did the curriculum:

I remember wondering why I should read Shakespeare when the Beats in America were writing all this exciting stuff and why I should listen to Beethoven when Eddie Cochrane was belting out rock and roll.

Eventually, Peter stopped going to lessons and was asked to leave the school. Lured by cheap travel and the easy availability of jobs, he took off for the United States. Over the next 18 months, as he hitch-hiked and worked his way around the country, he became acutely aware of racial tensions and of the poverty that lay beneath an outwardly prosperous society. At the time of his expulsion from school he had been a "rebel without a cause", aware of what he did not like about society but without any clear idea of what he wanted to take its place. By the time he returned to Britain early in 1964 he called himself a "socialist" and was committed to the struggle for a more just and equal society.

He had great hopes of the Labour government that was elected in October 1964:

It was a time of great optimism and faith in democracy. The scope of possibilities seemed endless. I remember being very, very interested at the time, not just in economic reform but in

15 Harold Wilson (right) on the morning after Labour's narrow election victory in October 1964. In the centre is deputy leader, George Brown, and, on the left, Mrs Wilson. The optimism soon dissolved into disillusion.

legal and educational reform as well. There were endless debates about the Open University, public schools versus state schools, comprehensivization, open-plan classrooms in primary schools. It all seemed tremendously exciting and *urgent*, for the government had a very small majority and every by-election was a cliff-hanger.

Disillusion quickly set in:

I remember being quite turned off by Harold Wilson's statement that he was just going to make capitalism work better. And the various economic crises showed us quite clearly that it was the City and the bankers who were still in charge rather than the Labour government.

When the Wilson government refused to grant independence to Southern Rhodesia (Zimbabwe) unless majority rule were established first, Ian Smith's all-white government announced a Unilateral Declaration of Independence (U.D.I.). Many Britons thought that armed force should be used to bring the rebels to heel, but Wilson would only go as far as imposing economic sanctions. This reluctance for an all-out battle against racism added to Peter's disenchantment:

I remember one ludicrous episode during the Rhodesian crisis when the Archbishop of Canterbury demanded his right to time on the air and appeared on television to warn all good Christians that they should be prepared for a holy war against Ian Smith. And literally the next shot was of Harold Wilson claiming his right to air time and saying that on no account would we actually *do* anything.

All in all, the policies of the Labour government seemed little different from those a Conservative government would have followed, and Peter rapidly lost faith in ordinary party politics and the tired old men who seemed to run them. He lived and worked in London between May 1965 and the summer of 1968 and mixed with the fringes of the radical youth movement:

We had a growing feeling that there must be an alternative outside traditional politics, although we had no clear idea of what that alternative was. I suppose it was very self-centred. There was such a cult of youth at the time – every politician worth his salt had to be photographed with his arm around Mick Jagger – that we genuinely saw youth as having the answer in some way, although I don't think any of us knew what the answer was.

The idea that violent opposition to the system was justifiable became fashionable. Peter himself dipped into the works of Marcuse, the German Marxist philosopher who had become the spokesman of the radical student left, although he found the style fairly incomprehensible. For ten heady days in May 1968 he believed that the French students might indeed topple de Gaulle's government:

16 The year of protest, 1968, in Britain. The police struggle with a demonstrator, one of 10,000 who gathered outside the American embassy in Grosvenor Square in October to demonstrate against the war in Vietnam.

We were all very excited by it. I knew people who went to Paris and lobbed bricks at the C.R.S. [riot police]. Some Parisian revolutionaries – at least they called themselves revolutionaries – stayed in our flat. I remember their long hair and red headbands.

When the French rebellion collapsed, there was still hope that others might carry on the struggle. In the autumn of 1968 Peter embarked on a four-year course at a teacher training college in Yorkshire. Some of his reasons for doing this were personal but he was partly spurred on by the belief that students were "it". During his first year there college life was dominated by radical politics:

There were so many political groups springing up – Anarchists, Trotskyists, Maoists – all seemed to be OK. And there was this strange body called the Revolutionary Socialist Students' Federation, which lasted no more than six or seven months and which met furtively in the rooms of sympathetic lecturers.

We were going to change the whole structure of education. We made serious demands that, as students were a majority at the college, they should also be a majority on the governing body, the academic board and the admissions board. We went on strike for a term in the summer of '69 and set up "alternative" seminars. And we set out to change the community around us. We set up playgroups, opened up the college to the local kids and formed community housing groups.

Within 12 months, however,

. . . the bubble had burst into what I call the Woodstock era. The big thing was drugs. It was not so much that everyone took them, but that drugs dominated the lifestyle – endless debates about how you smoked pot, which we called grass. Clothes became symbolic – long dresses, long hair and head bands. And the extraordinary language – imported black American slang.

Peter himself was "totally switched off by it all. It all seemed utterly false and pretentious". During his last three years at college he gave up active politics almost entirely.

Unlike some of his contemporaries, however, Peter Smith remained committed to the view that society needed a radical reform. He regarded the election of a Conservative government in 1970 with "utter revulsion". In the 1970s he resumed his political activity, this time in a more "realistic" way among the trade unions. In retrospect he regards the 1960s as

. . . a betrayal, by people like me, the 1960s rebels who were nearly all middle class, because in the end the rebellion veered away from its grass-roots. People who could have gone on to really change things settled for a joint and the music of Woodstock. . . . It was all self-indulgent, a sort of love of our own image. . . . It was a genuine cop-out and I certainly don't look back on it with any nostalgia.

Wilma King Hunter, the Black Experience

Wilma King Hunter was born in 1942 in the small town of Forest, Mississippi, in the heartland of the American South. She was raised in a society in which the inferior economic and legal status of Blacks had long been a fact of life. Public facilities were segregated along racial lines and those provided for Blacks were blatantly second-rate. The Forest swimming pool, for example, was open to Whites only and "there were a lot of people in that town who did not learn to swim – I was one of them – because there was just no place for us to go." Stores in downtown Jackson, the state capital, did not employ black salespersons, and many of the shops would not even allow black customers to try on clothes or shoes. Although segregation in public education had been outlawed by a Supreme Court decision in 1954, the high school that Wilma attended in Forest had still not been integrated by the time she left in 1960. Likewise, Jackson State College, from which she received her first degree in 1963, was a segregated institution. The more prestigious Mississippi State College (known locally as "Ole Miss") was reserved for Whites.

As a child, Wilma often resented these restrictions, but the pressures on her to accept the system as something that could not be changed were equally strong.

We were so well segregated until it was something that you were aware of but that you accepted as the way it was supposed to be. . . . It was a very small town and the pressures were there on you to toe the line because you knew that whatever you did was going to have repercussions on your parents.

Neither was there anything in Wilma's formal education that encouraged her to criticize her environment. High school classes had totally ignored the black experience in American history and the same was true of the courses at Jackson State.

While Wilma was an undergraduate, however, the mood of resignation among Southern Blacks was disappearing rapidly. One of her younger sisters failed to graduate from high school during this period: instead of attending classes regularly, she took to the streets in protest against the treatment meted out to Blacks. Mr King also became far more militant and kept a piece of lead piping in his car to use if he were harassed or assaulted in any way. Wilma herself was caught up in the new mood. She and a fellow student discovered a section of the Jackson State College Library that contained works by black authors. These they read and discussed together. The wife of James Meredith, the first black student to be admitted to Ole Miss, was a classmate of Wilma's and

. . . from time to time she would share her experiences with us. One of the things that she

17 James Meredith, accompanied by American marshals, goes to his first class at Ole Miss, 1 October 1962.

had were cardboard boxes of mail that people had written to her. Some of the mail was favourable, some of it was extremely violent and hostile.

Wilma herself was in a difficult position. The Jackson State College administration forbade political activity among its students on pain of expulsion, and many, including Wilma, chose to remain silent rather than jeopardize their futures. Upon graduation in the summer of 1963, however, she was freed from these restrictions and volunteered to do clerical work for the Jackson branch of the N.A.A.C.P. (National Association for the Advancement of Coloured People), whose field director was Medgar Evers. A fortnight later Evers was shot in the back outside his home:

This was an extremely moving and emotional thing for us because we had been typing for him one day and then to hear early next morning that he had been assassinated! He had a young child who was the classmate of one of my younger sisters, so she was extremely affected by the death of this child's father. When the funeral occurred there were demonstrations.

The same summer Wilma reached voting age and encountered some of the difficulties that Southern states placed in the path of Blacks trying to exercise their constitutional right:

We had to take a literacy test and that involved reading and interpreting a section of the Mississippi State Constitution. We copied it as it was printed and then interpreted the section. There was also a section of the Federal Constitution that had to be read, copied and interpreted. I passed the examination and then I had to pay a poll tax in order to be eligible to vote. . . . And a friend of mine who was a college graduate failed the examination, and she failed, not necessarily because she did not know the content or could not interpret the content, but because the registrar was the sole judge of who passed and who did not.

In 1963 and 1964 Wilma took part in an N.A.A.C.P.-sponsored boycott of stores that discriminated against Blacks. This action was to have a significant effect on her personal life:

If I hadn't participated fully in the boycott, I don't think I would have been able to go on to graduate school, because I did not purchase anything at all that year. . . . I just wore what I had and saved enough money from what I earned to put myself through school. If it had not been for the racial situation, I don't think I would have had the incentive to save as I did.

Consequently, in the autumn of 1964, Wilma King Hunter left her teaching job and enrolled as a graduate student at Indiana State University in Bloomington, Indiana. She was awarded a Masters degree in History in 1965.

In spite of the increasing self-awareness of Blacks, progress towards full civil rights in the South was painfully slow. Southern state governments devised some crafty strategems to avoid having to comply with the directives to desegregate sent out from Washington. The swimming pool in Forest, for example, was filled in and turned into a flowerbed rather than it being opened to all races. Wilma had gone to graduate school in Indiana, because in Mississippi the course she wanted to follow was only available at all-white colleges. After receiving her Masters degree, she moved to North Carolina and taught for two years in a small segregated college. When she moved into the state school system in 1967 desegregation in North Carolina was only just beginning. Wilma herself served on a committee to work out plans for integration.

Frustration spread among Blacks and many argued that the answer lay in adopting more violent tactics. Wilma sympathized with this view but believed that it would not work,

18 The alternative of violence. Two members of a ▶ militant black sect, the Black Panthers, Bobby Seale (left) and Huey Newton, in San Francisco 1969. Both were eventually arrested and imprisoned.

especially as Blacks were a minority among the population as a whole:

I could see that the militants probably got a lot more attention and probably would prod people to move faster in getting things done . . . but I decided that the original movements like the N.A.A.C.P. and the Southern Christian Leadership Conference were more practical in the sense that you would have a lot less black deaths with the non-violent movements than with the more militant ones. The Police Department in the City of Jackson had its heavy armament and it was not above bringing it out.

Nevertheless, much was achieved by the end of the 1960s, even though the achievement fell far short of the dream of complete political and economic equality. Through friends and family Wilma kept in touch with what was going on in Mississippi. Even there, by 1970,

The schools in Jackson had begun to desegregate, and I remember that in 1968 one of my sisters . . . was one of the first black teachers to work in Clinton, Mississippi, in the public school system. I feel fairly sure that inter-state transport had been desegregated and I feel reasonably sure that public transport within the city of Jackson had been integrated. The trains had also stopped using separate coaches. . . . In fact I remember my father [who was a railway worker] telling me that they had begun to modernize the train stations, and instead of having black waiting rooms and white waiting rooms they took the partitions down and had these large, open waiting rooms.

In the 1970s two of Wilma's younger sisters went on to attend the formerly all-white Mississippi Southern University, while the youngest sister took a degree in Chemistry from Ole Miss.

Wilma's own character was shaped by the times through which she lived. As a child she had noticed that the only black professional people in her small home-town were the teachers. She concluded, therefore, that for a black woman the road to a better life lay through education. In this she received

. . . a tremendous amount of encouragement from my immediate family, as well as from the community around me. . . . My parents were not college graduates or even high school graduates for that matter, but they knew that unless you went on you would have the same kinds of jobs they had had.

As a Black and as a woman, Wilma was to encounter many obstacles in her pursuit of a fulfilling career, and she is sure that the battles she had to overcome these obstacles (she eventually earned a doctorate in History and has gone on to teach at a number of American universities) played a significant role in developing her into a self-sufficient, determined and competent woman.

THE REVOLT OF YOUTH

"We fumbled, we floundered, and the worst thing is I still don't know how we should have handled it," confessed Clark Kerr, who had been president of the University of California at Berkeley during the first wave of student unrest there in September 1964, unrest that was to sweep through the campuses of the western hemisphere and Japan and reach a climax in 1968. This is hardly surprising, for the unrest was less about the specific grievances that triggered it off and which differed from campus to campus, than a symptom of the mood of the 1960s.

The 1950s had seen a dramatic expansion of higher education. Under the 1957–63 Conservative government in Britain seven new universities were planned. The student population in the United States increased in the same period from 1,676,851 to 3,042,220 and in France from 147,294 to 186,101. With so many young people living closely together it was perhaps inevitable that here the spirit of the 1960s appeared in its most intense form. It was, moreover, no coincidence that society's most violent critics should come not from the disadvantaged but from the affluent middle classes. Tom Hayden, a radical leader, explained in 1966:

In their upbringing, their parents stressed the right of children to question and make judgements. And then these students so often encountered social institutions that denied them their independence and betrayed the democratic ideals they had been taught. They saw that the men of learning were careerists; that school administrators and ministers almost never discussed the realities the students lived with; that even their parents were not true to the ideals they taught the young. (Quoted in M. Gentleman & D. Mermelstein, *The Great Society Reader*)

Radical ideas spread quickly from institution to institution. The writings of Guevara, Debray, Mao Tse-tung and Marcuse, all of whom argued in different ways that was permissible to use violence to overthrow repressive societies and bring about social change, became popular.

First to be attacked were the college authorities themselves, but the scope of the protest soon widened. Students at the Free University in West Berlin, staging a sit-in against a new regulation limiting the time available for student political activity, stressed that they were not just fighting this regulation but for the "realization of democratic freedom in all German society, of which the university is merely one element". American students took up the causes of black militants, Mexican farm workers, draft resisters, welfare mothers, reservation Indians and prisoners – both criminal and political. The Provos of Amsterdam launched the "White Bicycle" campaign to free the city centre from pollution by providing 50,000 cycles on loan to commuters. The Vietnam War became a major issue, and students everywhere attacked the symbols of American power in the shape of embassies and banks. American students burnt their draft cards or evaded call-up by fleeing abroad.

The fashion for protest spread beyond colleges. In 1968 pupils at lycées (high schools) all over France occupied their classrooms and demanded a greater say in the running of schools. Even primary school children were not untouched. At one junior school in southern England pupils organized a

protest march against bossy dinner ladies. They paraded with banners and sang the C.N.D. anthem "We Shall Not Be Moved".

The authorities were bewildered. Concessions on specific issues brought no respite, for the grievances of the young were directed at society as a whole. Retaliation, however, only bred further violence. When the West Berlin police tried to break up a demonstration against a visit by the Shah of Iran, a student, Benno Ohnesorg, was killed. Immediately, many students who had never taken any interest in politics became protesters and normal university life ground to a halt.

Others, inside and outside the colleges, sought a more meaningful life by opting out of regular society altogether. Sometimes the same individual tried both paths at different times. Eastern religions became popular, as did hallucinogenic drugs like L.S.D. and marijuana ("pot"), which were supposed to raise consciousness and provide an alternative way of viewing the world. Eastern cities like Katmundu and Kabul, where drugs were readily available, became places of pilgrimage. Thousands left their homes and schools to live in communes, which were supposed to be the bases of a new society. "Turn off", "tune in", "drop out", "make love not war", "do your

21 On the hippy trail. Young Westerners smoking "pot" in Katmandu, Nepal.

own thing" became the slogans of the day. The love lyrics of pop music gave way to protest songs and eulogies of the counter-culture. The climax came in August 1969, when 400,000 gathered at Woodstock in New York State for a three-day rock festival. To many it seemed as if once stable societies teetered on the verge of collapse.

In the end, it did not happen. As yet, it is only possible to speculate on the reasons why not. Young radicals were given a high profile by the media but were really only a minority

23 A student volunteer sorts out literature of the anti-war presidential candidate, Eugene McCarthy, in 1968. McCarthy hoped to capitalize on youthful disillusion with the established parties but failed to win more than a fraction of the vote.

among the population at large and won little popular support. In retrospect, many students of the time have come to realize the contempt in which they were held by members of the working class, who had to get up at six in the morning to go to their factories, had little

◀ **24** A conservative backlash in the United States. Nixon on the campaign trail in Southern California in 1968.

society as a whole. In most elections after 1968 voters chose politicians who could be depended on to restore traditional values. Thus Richard M. Nixon became President of the United States in 1968 and again in 1972, a Conservative government was elected with a landslide majority in Britain in 1970, and President de Gaulle of France, whose régime had seemed doomed in May 1968, appealed to the self-interest of the middle class and won the June election.

Psychological factors may also have played a part. Few could long sustain a life of such intensity. Daniel Cohn-Bendit, leader of the French students in 1968, admitted in his autobiography that he suffered from "burn-out". Jerry Rubin confessed in 1976:

I want to be politically active again – but not at the expense of my happiness and health. I do not want to be in a crazy movement that psychologically drains its people. (Quoted in C.K. Meinert, *Twilight of Youth*)

In time, most of the young rebels faded back into society, opting either for a private life or more traditional political activities. Those who could not conform found their way into the violent revolutionary groups like the Weathermen in the United States, the Red Brigade in Italy and the Baader-Meinhof Gang in West Germany, which periodically hit the headlines with acts of sabotage and kidnapping well into the 1970s.

energy left for all-night political discussions and could not risk being arrested in demonstrations. Only in France did a working alliance between factory workers and students emerge. It lasted barely three weeks. Those who sympathized with individual student demands such as an end to the war in Vietnam were often alienated by the violence or the use of drugs or the frequent attacks on adult

Sylvie T: France 1968

In May 1968 Sylvie T. was 18 years old and a first-year student at a Paris art academy. She

could not remember a time when she had not been dissatisfied with the society and politics

AU MUSÉE!..

...LE MONARQUE

CHARLES DE GAULLE RÉGNANTE (1958-1965)

25 General de Gaulle as Louis XIV. This cartoon, which appeared in the satirical newspaper *Le Canard Enchaîné*, captured the feelings of many French men and women about their president.

of de Gaulle's France. Although the system of government was technically democratic, the General's style was so autocratic that he was nicknamed "The Dictator" and "Louis XIV". Obsessed with foreign affairs, he paid little attention to social reform.

Throughout her high school days Sylvie had found it hard to channel her discontent constructively. For a while she had been a member of the Communist Party, which in France was an almost respectable part of the political system. She had left the party in disillusion as "it seemed to have little to offer idealistic young people". She found it "rigid and intolerant of any difference of opinion".

Even those among Sylvie's friends who were not interested in politics had grievances, for the social revolution that had already transformed British society had not spread across the Channel. French society and, in particular, its educational system were markedly authoritarian. At high school,

. . . teachers sat on a little stage like gods. We were called by our last names. Up until the age of ten or eleven we had to wear dreadful grey overblouses. I had teachers who made us walk into the classroom two by two like in the army . . . there was generally a great restlessness among students because of all this.

Among university students, in particular, there was a general feeling that "our futures were at stake but we were never consulted about our courses". The curriculum that Sylvie followed in her first year at art college seemed to her "absurd". There was no connection between "the way we were being educated and the demands of the world. Everything was so out of date." Great emphasis, for example, was laid on Renaissance sculpture but little or no attention was paid to modern abstract art or contemporary art history. By the spring of 1968 the majority of students that Sylvie knew were "very negative about the structure of our society and were ready to get involved in a movement like this just out of rebelliousness".

Sylvie attended classes in art history at the Sorbonne and was there on 3 May when the student revolt broke out. There had been a series of minor disturbances since the beginning of the year and a student leader, Daniel Cohn-Bendit, was due to be expelled for insulting a teacher. A group of students gathered to protest and the Dean, feeling overwhelmed, called the police. Sylvie saw

. . . a sea of policemen arriving, and it was the first time that anything like that had happened in France. Neither the police nor the army had ever been brought into the universities before. There was huge reaction. . . . It was quite spontaneous. It hadn't been prepared and it didn't, at the beginning, have any clear goals. It was just one big burst of rebellion. The student union called for a demonstration the next day to protest at what had happened and like everyone else I was surprised at how many people turned up. After that, every day more and more students would turn up at the Sorbonne to demonstrate. It just snowballed.

Fuelled by the students' example other sections of French society rose in revolt, although later events were to show that there were many different motives. Strikes and sit-ins began in factories. Professional groups like teachers, bank clerks and journalists walked out of their jobs. Lycée pupils occupied their schools and demanded sweeping reforms. The students themselves sealed off the areas around their colleges and declared them out of bounds to the police and university administrators. To defend their territory they set up barricades and fought battles with the police. By 22 May ten million workers were on strike and the normal life of the country had ground to a halt. It happened spontaneously and, for the most, part without the blessing of the official trade unions.

On 13 May, the tenth anniversary of de Gaulle's coming to power, Sylvie participated in the largest demonstration ever held in Paris. People of all ages and all walks of life marched under the slogan "Ten Years is Enough". Paris was "like a sea of people". The mood of daily life changed as more and more people realized that they had the power to change society:

People went down into the streets and just talked – that is one thing I remember most clearly about 1968 – people just connected in a way that had never happened before. It was unique. You'd get up in the morning and go down into the street

26 A meeting of strikers at the Renault factory near Paris, one of the first to join the short-lived alliance between workers and students in May 1968.

and there'd be a group of people arguing, sometimes extremely violently. . . . Everyone participated, even people who were against the movement. It was very joyful and not just among students. I didn't see it myself, but I heard that in the occupied factories there was also a very joyful atmosphere.

The rebellion had been unplanned, and no one had any clear idea of what the new society would be like. Everyone assumed, however, that it would be more truly democratic than the old. Anyone who wanted to would have a say in how things were run and people would have greater freedom to develop their own individual lifestyle. "Participation" became the catchphrase. Sylvie herself

. . . sat on a lot of committees . . . to discuss how to proceed with things. There was meeting after meeting. . . . Action Committees were organized to unite all the people in a particular area. You would have workplace committees and neighbourhood committees and a committee for each school at the university. I was on my neighbourhood committee and anyone who

27 A French student demonstrator emerging from a cloud of tear gas to throw a brick at the riot police, May 1968.

supported the movement could join. There was a lot of work – the daily chores of making a revolution – but we had lots of fun.

President de Gaulle soon called in the C.R.S., the riot police:

They were all over Paris. They were loathed by the population and very scary. There were checkpoints everywhere. Everyone was scared of that. It never happened to me but I knew quite a lot of people who were arrested and taken to the police station for no reason. . . . During demonstrations the C.R.S. were extremely brutal. I remember being very scared of being beaten up, and after a while we came to demonstrations equipped with helmets. Sometimes students being pursued by the police would escape into private houses and the police would follow and beat up everyone inside. I have to say, however, that the police were often deliberately provoked to the point where violence was inevitable.

Although sympathetic to the movement, Sylvie's parents were afraid for her safety and tried to discourage her from taking part in demonstrations.

For three weeks it appeared as if millions of French men and women were united in a drive to create a new society. Towards the end of the month, however, serious cracks began to appear in the movement. On 22 May trade union leaders announced their readiness to negotiate with the government over wage claims. Rumours began to circulate that de Gaulle was planning to call in French troops stationed in Germany to quell the revolt. On 27 May the trade unions accepted massive wage rises on behalf of their members and called off the factory occupations. All but a few groups of workers complied and the general strike collapsed. Sylvie felt

. . . incredible disappointment and shock. It didn't seem to make sense that the whole country could be shaken up like that and then it could just collapse. I felt completely bewildered. It seemed as if it had just erupted and then died. . . . Later I felt a lot of contempt for the cowardliness of the workers. They just didn't want to go to the end, they were afraid of change. In spite of everything, people were basically too comfortable to risk civil war.

Without mass support from the rest of the population the student movement slowly fizzled out.

Colleges and schools remained closed for the rest of the summer. When the autumn semester began most students went back to college as usual. There were some changes:

Relationships between students and teachers were changed for ever. I think that teachers felt that if they were too authoritarian it might trigger off another rebellion, and there was a tremendous desire to communicate, which was quite different from what it was before.

Orders had gone out from the government that educational institutions were to encourage student "participation". Sylvie served on a committee from her art college that visited the Ministry of Education to discuss the content of courses. These reforms, however desirable, fell far short of the sweeping changes dreamed of by the May rebels, and some of the more radical students refused to have anything to do with them on the grounds that they were a "sell-out" to the government. Sylvie herself felt "depressed, as if it had all been for nothing".

Between 1968 and 1970 she completed her degree but never really shook off the feeling of despondency:

I remember it as a grey, depressing time, although I don't know if that was just my personal perception or something to do with the spirit of the time.

She did notice, however, that a number of her friends went abroad, especially to Nepal and North Africa, and wondered to what extent

. . . there was a general feeling of wanting to escape. These were the years of the hippie movement, which was also caused by disillusion with the society we lived in. People who were disappointed by the failure of 1968 may have been looking for a kind of romantic escape. I took a different route.

In 1971 Sylvie received a scholarship to study in the United States. Finding there a more stimulating and less oppressive society, she never returned permanently to France again. In the long term, however, she did not feel that the rebellion of 1968 was either unjustified or ineffective:

I don't believe any more that there is a simple solution to the problems of society. The world is much too complex . . . that was the naïvety of youth and the naïvety of the era . . . but I don't feel the need to regret what I did. . . . In 1968 there was a profound need for action to move France forward. Now when I visit, French society seems to get more open every year, but I don't think this liberalization would have been achieved without a violent upheaval, a sort of shock to the system. Given the context of 1968, I would do it again, for it had to happen if France was to move forward into a new era.

John, an Australian Hippie

In 1970 an English sociologist interviewed a number of young people, mainly in their early twenties, who were living in communities in the Ladbroke Grove and Notting Hill areas of London. All had, to a greater or lesser degree, "dropped out" of regular society in an attempt to find a more satisfactory lifestyle. The interviews were published in 1971 in R. Mills, *The Young Outsiders: A Study of Alternative Communities.* Here is the story, told in his own words, of John, an Australian hippie.

John (his real name was not used by the author to protect his privacy) was born in Tasmania, an island off the coast of Australia, which was culturally part of the Western world. As he reached his late teens, he became aware of just how isolated his community was from the mainstream of the 1960s:

Every day I would read in the local paper the events that took place in far-off places like England and America and even in Australia. I became fairly convinced that my local paper wasn't telling it as it was, especially when I became particularly interested in Indonesia and met some students from there.

About this time too echoes of Bob Dylan could be discerned, and a group called the Beatles began to overrun the world – but it was all happening over there – in England or America, and nothing continued to happen in Tasmania.

At 18 he took a job in a bank, which he grew to loathe. Thus began a process of rejecting his parents' society in search of an identity of his own. At first he tried the fast life, in which he

. . . regularly got drunk and dragged around the town looking for women and parties with my friends, and always got into financial difficulties because I believed that I had to fix every dent I put in my car, which was my entire life.

It didn't work. "Something inside me was denied." He moved to the mainland and here for the first time he came into contact with hippies and the drug scene. At the same time, in search of meaningful work, he took a job with a mining company on an Aboriginal reserve and came to the conclusion that "primitive peoples have more to teach us than we have to teach them about how to live". In November 1969, therefore, John flew to Indonesia, where he discovered

. . . friendly, unspoiled people who seemed to live in perfect harmony. I was completely overwhelmed by their generosity and hospitality. They were the most happy, contented, uninhibited people I have ever seen.

For three months I travelled in Indonesia and the impression it made on me will never be erased . . . their entire nature seemed to be a complete contradiction to everything wrong with my own country and presumably the Western world.

At the same time, he took up the regular smoking of hashish (pot), which was commonly believed to release inhibitions and raise consciousness. Moving to Singapore, he experienced "what worked out to be a culmination of all previous experiences". During the Chinese New Year festivities,

All of a sudden I was exposed to myself and at

33

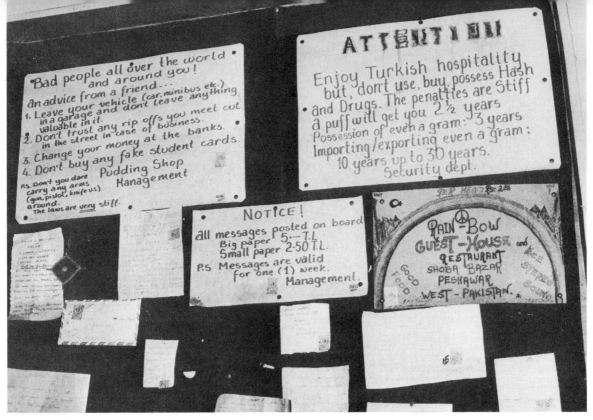

28 The notice board in an Istanbul restaurant, the first major stop on the hippy trail to the East.

29 A hippy "love-in" in London's Hyde Park in July 1967 to celebrate the acquittal of the Rolling Stones pop group on drugs charges. ▼

AROUND THE WORLD

When we study the past we search for themes that will make it more comprehensible to us. Often, however, developments do not fit neatly into a single mould. While the Western world was struggling with the problems of affluence, important events were taking place elsewhere in the world, stemming from quite different causes and operating on a different timescale.

In the Communist world the period of hope and change that is the nearest equivalent to 1960 took place between the years 1953 and 1956, when Stalin's death had awoken hopes of an end to the police state. To a certain extent, this had happened. Much of Stalin's apparatus of terror was dismantled by his successor, Khrushchev, and, in spite of the savage suppression of the Hungarian uprising in 1956, the satellite states of Eastern Europe were given some economic and cultural

33 A road being laid through a residential area of Novoyi Cheremushki in the Soviet Union in 1964. In Eastern Europe the hardships of the 1940s and early 1950s were giving way to greater affluence.

34 The trial of Sinyavsky and Daniel. The short-lived liberalization of the Khrushchev years had began to evaporate by 1966.

freedom. Everywhere behind the Iron Curtain the standard of living rose immeasurably. The dream of greater freedom inside the Soviet Union itself, however, did not materialize. Censorship was tightened again after 1962, culminating in the trial and imprisonment of two writers, Yuli Daniel and Andrei Sinyavsky, in 1966. In January 1968 the eyes of the world turned to Czechoslovakia, where liberal Communists led by Alexander Dubcek had seized control of the party and set about democratizing Czech public life. They called it "socialism with a human face". The hopes of the "Prague Spring" were shattered, however, when Russian tanks invaded Czechoslovakia on 20 August 1968.

In 1966, under the slogan "there can be no construction without destruction", Mao Tse-tung, Chairman of the Chinese Communist Party, announced the opening of the Great Proletarian Cultural Revolution. At the time, few Westerners fully understood what was happening, but it has since become clear that Mao, fearful that China was losing its revolutionary purity and fervour, set out to purge the country of all traces of "bourgeois" culture. His agents were the youthful Red Guards, whom he recruited by closing down the schools. For a while, the then prime minister Chou En-lai later confessed, the country was on the verge of civil war. In the end, the army was called in to restore order. At the same time, China arrived on the world stage as a great power. In 1960 she quarrelled publicly with her ally, the Soviet Union, and there were serious border clashes between them in 1963 and 1969. In 1962 China came out on top in a war with India and in 1964 she exploded her first atom bomb.

In the Middle East the long-standing emnity between Israel and her Arab

35 Israeli tanks advancing during the Six-Day War, ▶ which brought the Arab-Israeli dispute into the centre of the world stage.

neighbours flared up once again into open warfare. In the Six Day War, 5–11 June 1967, Israel seized a further 26,000 square miles of Arab territory. The Palestinian refugees, driven from their homes, formed El Fatah (Palestine Liberation Organization), which wages guerilla war against Israel to the present day.

To the black African states that became independent during the 1960s fell the difficult task of establishing prosperity and stability. From the beginning, the new nations were plagued by tribal rivalries, climatic disasters, fluctuating commodity prices and shortages of skilled manpower, and by 1970 both prosperity and political stability seemed as far away as ever. Many states had suffered one or more military coups, and civil war had broken out in the Congo (Zaïre) in 1960–4 and Nigeria in 1967–70. The history of the few

36 U.D.I. in Southern Rhodesia. Mr Clifford Dupont, a member of the all-white Rhodesia Front government, is sworn in as "Acting Officer adminstering the Country" in place of the British governor, Sir Humphrey Gibbs. The country was to be ruled by its white minority until 1980.

37 Sharpeville, South Africa, 1960.

remaining white-ruled states was hardly less eventful. When Britain refused to give Southern Rhodesia (Zimbabwe) independence without majority rule, Southern Rhodesia declared U.D.I. South Africa's Apartheid policy and the 1960 massacre at Sharpeville, in which police fired into a crowd of unarmed Blacks demonstrating against the Pass Laws and killed 180 of them, led to her expulsion from the British Commonwealth in 1961. Strong emotions were aroused in 1964 when the black nationalist leader, Nelson Mandela, was imprisoned for life. While the majority of black South Africans still confined themselves to peaceful protests, a growing minority, particularly among the young, argued that racial justice would only be achieved by violence. The Nigerian war disturbed the conscience of the world when news leaked out in 1968 of a severe famine which was killing and handicapping thousands of children in the rebel state of Biafra. In the Portuguese colonies of Guinea, Angola and Mozambique, which Portugal refused to give up, guerilla armies were beginning an armed struggle for independence. None of these problems was near a solution when the decade ended.

◄ **38** The victims of war. A Biafran woman begging by the side of the road.

Jiang Zhi: the Cultural Revolution in China

Jiang Zhi was born into a middle-class family in 1944 and grew up under the Communist régime that took over the country in 1949. Although the family had to adjust its lifestyle to fit into the new China, Jiang Zhi's boyhood memories are happy and hopeful. He was an excellent student and in 1962 won a place at the prestigious Peking Institute of Foreign Languages. He remembers the next four years as his "golden age". From his studies of English language and culture he felt that a whole new world had been opened up to him. He had great ambitions for the future:

Ours was a special group and we learned that probably one quarter of the students in our group would be sent to England [to pursue postgraduate studies at Oxford and Cambridge], another quarter would be sent to embassies in Western countries, and another half or so would continue advanced studies in this school.

With shocking suddeness all these dreams were shattered:

1 June [1966] was a weekday and early in the morning everything was normal. I got up and did morning exercises, went to the canteen and had my breakfast and then went back to the dormitory to get my things ready for morning classes. It was 6.30 a.m. – that was the time all the radio stations in China broadcast the national news, exactly the same across the whole country – and that day something unusual seemed to be going on so I listened very hard. We were told that a great new revolution was beginning and that everyone should support it wholeheartedly.

The following day came the news that the students at the University of Peking had stopped their classes so that they could devote their time to the Great Proletarian Cultural Revolution. "And on the afternoon of the very same day," recalled Jiang Zhi, "the heads of our school gave their decision and school had to be stopped." Higher education in China

39 Mao Tse tung (Mao Zedong) (front right) is greeted with adulation by young Chinese Red Guards, many of whom are carrying the "Little Red Book", Bible of the Cultural Revolution.

was not to return to something like normal for over three more years.

Communist Party officials spoke to the students and gave out copies of *The Thoughts of Chairman Mao* – the so-called "Little Red Book". They were told:

Search the memory to see if the professors have said anything that is not in keeping with Chairman Mao's teachings. . . . Compare what you learned, compare what you heard, compare what you were taught with the book.

Teachers whose revolutionary fervour was called into question were branded as "bourgeois intellectuals" and ruthlessly humiliated. Very soon, anyone who had more than an elementary education, who had studied Western culture or who owned Western goods was under suspicion. At the Peking Institute in the middle of June, for example, some students

. . . went to the rooms of a very well-known professor of English, who had majored in English at Oxford or Cambridge. He lived on the fourth floor and they threw dictionaries, Shakespeare plays, all his papers and writings out of the window. At the last moment, when they were about to leave, they threw a large pot of goldfish out of the window. It all seemed so senseless.

Jiang Zhi himself was never really taken in by the new ideology. It seemed to him that it was the younger, less mature students who were won over, while those like himself who were about to graduate were more sceptical and often "disgusted" by the persecution of elderly teachers. One incident above all was decisive in shaping his attitude towards the Cultural Revolution. All graduating students at the Institute had been issued with a report card listing their gradings throughout the four-year course. Jiang Zhi was particularly proud of his, with its final mark of 5–5 (double A). Then,

One day all the students in my grade, about a hundred or so, were told to take their cards and

go to the sportsfield. They started a fire and everyone threw their record into the fire. I was about to cry but I couldn't. I was suffocating. It was one of the most miserable moments of my life. I had worked so hard for all this. This little book meant so much to me, but I had to swallow my tears. That's why, later, even when this lie was repeated hundreds of times and I was a little bit taken in by the whole ideology I had no stomach for it – that was not because of my political standpoint but because of my personal feelings.

Whatever his personal inclinations, Jiang Zhi had little choice but to pay lip-service to the ideals of the Cultural Revolution. Once, at the beginning, when he voiced his disquiet, he was told by one of his teachers: "Don't say anything about politics; don't voice any disapproval. Keep it to yourself." When students were sent out of Peking to spread the revolution to the provinces Jiang Zhi was forced to go along. He participated as little as possible, however, and took this opportunity to do some sightseeing in areas of China he'd never visited before. As the Cultural Revolution deepened, the process of "re-education" took a new turn. To rid themselves of their "bourgeois" thought-patterns, intellectuals were ordered to "redeem" themselves through manual labour. Some were sent to collective farms, some into mines and factories. Jiang Zhi was drafted into the army, where he found himself despised by the ordinary soldiers as a "filthy intellectual". On one occasion, as he and some companions were on their way to a bath-house in a neighbouring village, they were threatened by a pack of ferocious dogs. To frighten the dogs off, they threw lumps of clay at them. The dogs turned out to be military watchdogs and the regular soldiers hauled Jiang Zhi and his friends before the division commander. He still remembers with bitterness,

◀ **41** Reading big character posters in Canton. This was one way in which the latest official line was communicated to the ordinary Chinese.

Most of the soldiers were illiterate people from the countryside who knew nothing at all. They just scorned intellectuals and I was very upset. We felt that we intellectuals were even cheaper than a dog.

Jiang Zhi was not the only member of his family whose life was disrupted by the Cultural Revolution. His younger brother, who was also a brilliant student, was dispatched to a state farm on the northern frontier of China and lost the chance of going to university:

Life there was really very miserable for him. For one thing because of the weather, for another because of the food, which was entirely but also because the people on the farm were illiterate and kept these city people working so hard.

Not only education, but also China's economic life was disrupted:

Agrarian products were not greatly affected because probably the Revolution did not run as rampant in the countryside as it did in the cities. The cities were really affected – you could hardly buy soap or detergent or sugar or matches – anything to do with industry. They were all highly rationed.

By 1970 Jiang Zhi noticed that the pace of the Cultural Revolution was slowing down. At the end of that year he was discharged from the army and assigned as a teacher to a high school near Shanghai. This marked something of an improvement in the humanity of official attitudes, as it enabled Jiang Zhi to live near his family home. However, it was not until the death of Mao in 1976 and the downfall of the Gang of Four that the stigma against intellectuals was fully removed and Jiang Zhi was able to get work commensurate with his qualifications. In 1979 he entered a post-graduate programme at Shanghai Teachers' University, eventually being appointed a teacher there. In 1984 he became Director of Linguistic and Literary Research. Ironically, the almost total shut-down of higher education during the Cultural Revolution worked ultimately to Jiang Zhi's benefit. By the early 1980s there was such a shortage of younger educated people that at last "we middle-aged intellectuals got our chance".

Although the 40 years of Jiang's life have spanned four momentous decades in Chinese history it is the period of the Cultural Revolution that he sees as the most significant influence on his life:

Even today I can't believe this happened to me. You see, every time I had something unpleasant, something upsetting in my life, I thought, "If this revolution had not come, I would not have had so much trouble, so many miserable things in my life."

Nguyen Thi Lan, a Vietnamese Peasant

In 1965, as the war in South-East Asia was hotting-up, Susan Sheehan, wife of a foreign correspondent with *The New York Times*, decided to interview some ordinary Vietnamese, for

. . . to me their absence from most accounts of the war seemed regrettable. It was these Vietnamese – the people I've called the 95% that don't count – who interested me, for the war is being fought over them and they are its chief participants and its chief victims.

Her interviews were published in New York in 1967 as *Ten Vietnamese*. One of her subjects was Nguyen Thi Lan (not her real name), a grandmother of 56, who had lived all her life in An Binh hamlet, a village of about 100 huts in the fertile, rice-growing Mekong Delta.

Lan is still a slender woman, about five feet tall. She wears her black hair pulled straight back from her forehead and tied in a small bun at the back. Her customary attire is a pair of billowing black satin trousers and a well-patched white

42 The victims of war. Vietnamese civilian refugees being airlifted by an American helicopter from their homes in the battle zone to a safer area. ▶

cotton overblouse; she usually goes barefoot but wears a glazed conical hat when she goes outside. Her face and arms are wrinkled from years of work and exposure to the sun.

She had never been to school and rarely left her village, even to go to Saigon, the capital, three hours' drive away. Life was always precarious. In a good year Lan and her husband grew enough rice to feed a family of nine (the youngest daughter, a son, his wife and four children lived with them) and pay the rent. In a bad year, when the rains failed, they had to beg the landlord to lower the rent. If a disaster such as illness struck, they were forced to go into debt to neighbours or money-lenders.

From 1945 the hamlets of the Mekong Delta had been the scene of intermittent civil war, firstly (1945–54) between French colonial troops and Vietnamese Communist guerillas, the Vietminh; and then, from 1956, between the American-backed government of South Vietnam and the Vietcong, who wanted to unify the South with the Communist North. An Binh's fortunes fluctuated. Until 1964 it was under the control of the Vietcong; in December 1964 it was brought under government control, although still subject to raids by the Vietcong. Susan Sheehan asked Lan what she felt about the war raging around her. Of the French war Lan said: "We didn't take sides. We didn't understand what the fighting was all about. We were only interested in our field work." When the French left she was happy because "the

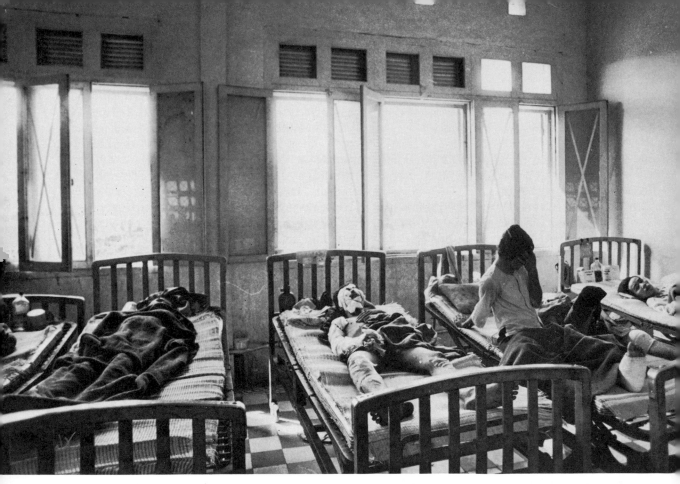

hamlet became quiet again". Of Lan's reaction to the current war Susan Sheehan wrote:

Lan has heard the term Vietcong but she does not know what Communism is and she refers to the guerillas either as the "Viets". . . or as "liberation people". She refers to the government soldiers and officials as "nationalist people". She understands the new war vaguely as a struggle for the leadership of the country between the nationalist people and the liberation people. She knows the Americans are helping the nationalist people but she doesn't know why. She has not heard of anyone helping the liberation people. . . . "Russia" and "China" mean nothing to her.

Most of Lan's neighbours were, like her, pawns in a war beyond their comprehension. Some families had sons on both sides, and often this depended on which group had occupied the hamlet when that particular son reached draft age. "Taking sides",

43 The victims of war. Civilian casualties in a South Vietnamese hospital.

commented Lan, "is largely a matter of taste and chance. I wouldn't join either side myself."

The peasants could not, however, opt out of the war altogether. One night in 1964 bullet holes were made in the wall of Lan's hut, and the same year one of her sons was badly injured when he stepped on a Vietcong landmine. Just before the interview took place, the Vietcong had raided the village again and killed two civilians. When she heard what was going on, Lan hid under her bed until it was all over.

Both sides in the Vietnam conflict would have probably argued that the object of the struggle was to create a system that would lift peasants like Lan out of ignorance and poverty. What Lan's testimony bears out, however, is that those on whose behalf a war is fought may turn out to be its chief victims. Let Lan have the last word:

I can't afford to resent the Vietcong because my son's injury is beyond my control. It's useless to be angry. It's a waste of emotion. I have to bear the consequences of the war but I can't do anything about it. I might as well save my words and feelings.

I would like the war to end because I hate hearing shooting and artillery and planes and bombs. I don't like to find bullet holes in my walls. I'm very much afraid of being killed when there is shooting. I'm planning to dig a hole to take refuge in. I'm always anxious and tense. I can't sleep well at night. When there's shooting, you never know if you'll get hit or killed. I've heard that a bomb was dropped on a hamlet somewhere near here the other day. A couple of people were killed and all their furniture was damaged. But my fieldwork is not affected by the war. If the crops are good I can make ends meet. If not I have to beg the landlord to lower the rent and borrow some money so that my family will have enough to eat.

Vera L: Czechoslovakia 1968

Vera L was born in 1947, a year before the Communists took power in Czechoslovakia, and spent the first 21 years of her life under a dictatorship that allowed little freedom of thought or expression. At school, compulsory courses in Political Sciences, History and Economics fed children with a one-sided view of Czech history, in which the Communist Party and the Soviet Union could do no wrong. Those who suspected that they were being given a distorted view had no means of discovering the truth for themselves, for all publications were strictly censored, as was radio and television. Moreover, it was dangerous to discuss doubts, even among friends, for the secret police had spies everywhere. At home, Vera's father, a long-time Party member, foiled any attempts by his children to question the Party line. When her elder brother, Jan, tried to draw their father into an argument, he was always gently fobbed off, which made him furious.

None of this worried Vera much. She found politics boring and could not understand why some of her friends would gather furtively in corners during lunch breaks to discuss forbidden things. "Nothing will ever change," she thought, "so why bother?"

In spite of the repressive atmosphere of the 1950s and early 1960s, the Communist régime had succeeded in establishing a decent standard of living for most people. Free university education was readily available, the only condition being that students were politically "reliable". In 1966, therefore, Vera enrolled at the university in her home town of Brno. Even for foreign language students like Vera political courses were compulsory and their content was drearily familiar:

I didn't really listen to the content at all. I regarded it as just another exam to pass. I learned what I had to off by heart and then forgot it all afterwards.

During her second year there, however, a new wind began to blow through Czechoslovakia. In January 1968 Antonin Novotny, who had been Party Secretary since 1953, was ousted and his place taken by Alexander Dubcek. Over the next six months the apparatus of repression was rapidly dismantled and people were able to publish and criticize with a freedom unknown since 1939 (the year of the German invasion). While insisting that Czechoslovakia would remain a Communist state and an ally of the Soviet Union, Dubcek and his colleagues talked of

44 Socialism with a human face. Alexander Dubcek talking with Czechs in the street on his way to work in the morning.

"socialism with a human face". Vera remembers:

Suddenly everyone was talking politics quite openly. I had a boyfriend who wasn't interested in anything else – he was always at a meeting or on his way to one. I didn't really follow all the ins and outs, but even I was infected by the new atmosphere. The ingrained fear of authority that had always been part of our lives, the habit of always looking over your shoulder to see who might be listening, disappeared. It was like being drunk – you wanted to say outrageous things just to prove that you were free to say them.

With the benefit of hindsight, Vera believes that the enthusiasm of the Czech people for their new-found freedom pushed the leadership into moving faster than they thought wise:

There were a lot of demonstrations that spring, even though they were peaceful, good-natured ones. During the warm nights of early summer no one seemed to sleep. The area outside our dormitory was often full of students demanding more democracy and carrying pictures of Dubcek and Svoboda [the president]. Everyone regarded Dubcek as a kind of saint – a Communist who was also a decent human being, who really cared about people's opinions – not just a faceless bureaucrat who knew what was best for you. But by the end I think he was being swept along by forces beyond his control.

Not everyone was intoxicated by what was happening. Many old-time Communists like Vera's father feared that greater freedom might undermine the control of the Party and open the way to counter-revolution and the destruction of all that had been achieved since 1948. The Russians, too, feared that the "Prague Spring" would weaken Czechoslovakia's loyalty to Communism and threaten the Soviet Union's own security.

On the night of 20–1 August 1968 Russian, East German, Polish and Bulgarian troops invaded. As the tanks entered Brno at 4 a.m., Vera woke up and went up on to the roof of her dormitory to see what was happening:

Thousands of planes were flying overhead and tanks were roaring by below. It was so early in the morning that it was still misty and everything had an unreal quality, as if we were watching a film. Then one of the tanks pointed its guns at us and told us to get down or they would shoot – so we did.

To avoid bloodshed and in the vain hope of Western intervention, Dubcek's government ordered its citizens to offer only passive resistance to the invaders. For the next few days the mood remained strangely buoyant:

The Russian soldiers were mostly young country boys and totally ignorant. Many had no clear idea why they were here, and some even thought they were in West Germany or Israel! It seemed that we only had to explain things to them and the entire army would fall apart and have to pack up and go home. Our government

45 The end of a dream. A Soviet tank in front of the statue of King Wenceslaus in Prague, August 1968. The statue is daubed with the names of Dubcek and Svoboda.

had told us that on no account were we to use physical force, so crowds gathered around all the tanks in the street and talked to the soldiers, explaining patiently that there was no counter-revolution in Czechoslovakia and that the Russian comrades had got it all wrong. . . . I didn't talk myself, but I went with those who did. It was strange, but we were so convinced that justice was on our side that we weren't at all depressed. It was the Russian soldiers who seemed worried and confused.

At home, however, things were tense:

As a family we were normally quiet and restrained. It was quite a shock when I heard my brother shout at my father: "See what your lot

have gone and done to us!" My father brought out the standard line about the Russian troops being here to defend us, but I don't think he really believed it. It was as if his whole world had been turned upside down.

In time, reality intervened. No help arrived from the West and there was no way that a nation of eight million people could prevail for long against the armed might of the Soviet Union and her allies. After a week the young conscripts were replaced by more reliable career soldiers:

We were all afraid of *them*. I used to cross over on to the other side of the street as they went by. Fraternization ceased, and it began to sink in that this was the beginning of the end.

46 Hopeless defiance. Posters caricaturing the Russians on a shop window in Prague, 1968.

When the university term re-opened in the autumn, the Russians and their Czech supporters were firmly in charge. The mood of the students was depressed, and lecturers who in the spring had encouraged political debate in the classroom had become noticeably more cautious. Over the next year many of the more outspoken teachers were replaced by more compliant ones, and political classes became drearily predictable once again. This pattern reflected what was happening in society at large, where all institutions, including the Party, were gradually purged of those who had supported the Prague Spring – a process known as "normalization".

As she had been an onlooker rather than an active participant, Vera's academic career continued unhindered, although in the excitement of the spring she had failed some of her exams and had to resit the following year. Some of her friends, however, were hounded out of the university, and Jan, who had a degree in Physics, was turned down for all the jobs that matched his qualifications and forced to earn his living as a janitor. When Vera left Czechoslovakia in 1970, however, it was not, as it was for many others, for political reasons but for personal ones. In that year she met and married a foreign student and was allowed to settle permanently abroad.

LIVING THROUGH THE 1960s

Most people do not make history, they live through it. This was true even in the 1960s, when public awareness of political and social issues was unusually high. It was also, however, the decade in which the mass media came of age. Most households in the West now possessed a television, and in 1962 Telstar, the first of the communications satellites that were to make it possible to relay pictures round the globe almost instantaneously, was launched. For the first time ever, few people could fail to be aware of what was going on around them. And most of the cultural changes, which permanently altered Western societies, would not have been possible if the majority of ordinary citizens had not come to accept them.

47 A Berlin street divided down the middle by the building of the Wall, August 1961. People stranded on the wrong side of the wall were permanently cut off from their homes and families.

People's sense of what was important differed. For some, it was a decade of high hopes and deep disappointment. Although much of the Kennedy image has since been exposed as a myth, at the time he was idolized by many. There are few people who were alive then who do not remember clearly what they were doing at the moment that news of his assassination broke. For the young, 1968 was an apocolyptic year. Romantic hopes of revolution were shattered by the Soviet invasion of Czechoslovakia, the collapse of the May Revolution in France, the election of Nixon.

Others remember the violence and insecurity – the building of the Berlin Wall in 1961, which divided the city and split up families; the Cuban Missile Crisis of 1962, when the world seemed on the verge of a nuclear war; the assassinations of Robert Kennedy, Martin Luther King and Malcolm X; the wounding of the German student leader, Rudi Dutschke. Days before the opening of the Olympic Games in Mexico City in October 1968 the Mexican police opened fire on demonstrators in the city centre and killed 33, including a 60-year-old woman and a three-year-old boy. All over Europe, American embassies became the target of demonstrations. Millions sat by their television screens and watched the racial violence of the "long hot summers" of 1965–9 or the Chicago police beating up demonstrators at the 1968 Democratic Convention. When the black American athletes who won first and third places in the 200 metres dash at the Mexico Olympics gave the Black Power salute during the playing of the "Star Spangled Banner" (the American national anthem) it seemed to many as if civilization was about to collapse in chaos.

No one could fail to be aware of the dramatic cultural changes that swept away old certainties in dress and behaviour. In Britain, the unsuccessful prosecution of Penguin

48   A violent decade. Malcolm X, the black leader, on the floor of the Audubon Ballroom in New York seconds after being shot, February 1965.

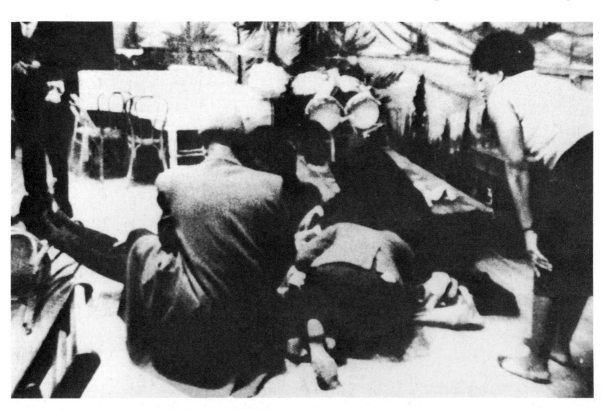

49 A still from *The Knack*, one of the sexually explicit films of the 1960s. ▶

Books for issuing an unabridged version of *Lady Chatterly's Lover* opened the way for a rapid loosening of censorship. By the end of the decade nudity and "four letter words" (as they were squeamishly called) were common on stage and in films. The hit musical of 1968, "Hair", which extolled the joys of the hippie life, had both. Perhaps the most remarkable feature of the decade was the way in which changes that had seemed shocking at the beginning – the length of the Beatles' hair, coloured shirts for businessmen, caricatures of the British royal family – seemed unremarkably tame by the end, so rapidly had society changed. Parents who had criticized first the Beatles and then the Rolling Stones remembered both with nostalgia when faced with The Who and Jimi Hendrix.

Others were fascinated by the technological advances of the age – the first man in space in 1961; the first moon-landing in 1969; the first heart transplant performed by Dr Christian

50 The first men on the moon, July 1969.

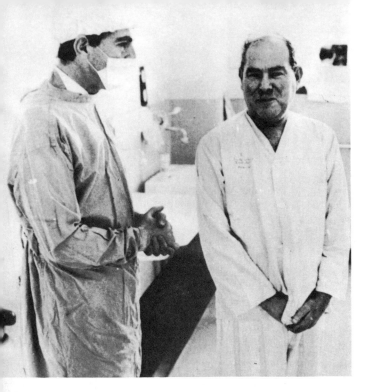

51 Technological breakthrough. Dr Christian Barnard and Philip Blaiberg, the world's first successful heart transplant patient, in Cape Town, 1968.

Barnard in South Africa in 1967; even the proliferation of cheap transistor radios.

Even those who disapproved of much that was going on tend to regard the 1960s as a uniquely unforgettable era. The older sisters of Diane, whose story appears on pages 63-6, often criticized the music she played. Now, however, they refer to it with indulgence. There are few who lived through the decade who do not have something to say about it – for good or for ill.

Betsy Tompkins, an American Housewife

For most of the 1960s Betsy and Howard Tompkins lived and worked near the big cities of America's East Coast. From 1961 to 1967 they lived in Bethesda, Maryland, which served as a dormitory suburb for Washington's politicians and bureaucrats. In 1967 they moved to North White Plains in New York State, and Howard commuted daily to a research job in New York City. One by one, between 1963 and 1970, the four Tompkins daughters passed through the American college system. The lives of all six family members, therefore, were touched by the events that shook American society during that decade.

Betsy was excited by Kennedy's election in November 1960:

We felt that at last we were going to have someone who had youth, hope, idealism. . . . I was a Kennedyite! I watched the debates on television and followed the campaign as much as I could. I was just thrilled when he got in.

His assassination in 1963 was a shock so great that Betsy remembers her initial reaction as if it had occurred yesterday:

I walked into a card shop and it [the news of the assassination] was on the radio. I thought it was one of those terrible productions like Orson Welles' "War of the Worlds". I turned to the owner and said, "They shouldn't have things like that on the radio. It's just ridiculous." And he looked at me and said, "I'm sorry, it's not ridiculous, it's true." I ran home and turned on the radio there

52 Stunned Americans looking at the latest bulletin on President Kennedy's shooting, 22 November 1963. ▶

and listened and listened and just couldn't believe it.

It was, moreover, more than just a shock:

It just seemed to take some of the light out of the air for so many of us because we had looked forward to so much. I don't know, perhaps we would have been disappointed, but from then on the atmosphere around us, politically, was never the same.

This impression was heightened by the fact that Betsy disliked the new President, Lyndon Johnson. She thought him "crude, very unpresidential, an opportunist who thought more of his own position than of what was really going to happen and what good it was going to do".

Betsy and Howard were Quakers and had their doubts about the morality of the Vietnam War from the beginning, long before such opposition became widespread. This often put them at odds with their neighbours. People who were "friends at first were likely to turn on us when they found out that we were doves (people who opposed the war. Those who supported it were called 'hawks'.) We had to be very careful because we didn't want any damage to the house or the car." In the early

53 Anti-war demonstrators burn draft records in Milwaukee, 1968.

days, Betsy sometimes had doubts about her stand, but these were soon swept away by a personal encounter:

I remember listening to a French journalist, Bernard Fall, who had come to Washington to explain to Americans why we couldn't achieve anything in Vietnam. I talked to his wife and she said, "He's going back and I don't think he will ever come back to me." Two weeks later he was killed in Vietnam. We had liked him so much that it hurt and we couldn't explain to people, no one seemed to listen to what he had said.

Betsy's daughters lived through the growing unpopularity of the war among students, and the second daughter, herself a devout Quaker, became involved in anti-war protests at the University of Arizona. On one occasion, late in 1968, she and some fellow students, mostly girls, went to the support of a boy who was publicly burning his draft card in front of a hostile crowd. The incident was filmed by a television crew and that evening Betsy received a telephone call from her daughter, telling her parents not to be anxious if they should see her on the news. In fact, that particular news footage was never used. The third daughter, Wendy, failed to graduate on schedule from Oberlin College for what Betsy felt were blatantly political reasons:

She was the truck driver for a group that went down to Washington to march. . . . When she came back one of her papers was one day late and she flunked the course. Some professors found it difficult to be flexible enough to cope with the confusion and the needs of students during that time.

None of the girls became actively involved in the rebellion against American society that swept through the colleges in the late 1960s, but the youngest daughter, Vicki, who graduated from Radcliffe (part of Harvard University) in 1970, could not but be affected by it. Student life was often disrupted by militants, who tried to occupy administrative offices and classrooms, destroy records and harass professors with unpopular views. One night, when Betsy was visiting Vicki:

There were 3000 who just rampaged through the square smashing things. My second daughter's future father-in-law, who was a Dean, was down in the square trying to calm the Harvard students who were there. We were all gathered around the T.V. worrying about him because Vicki had warned us there was going to be trouble and she hoped he would not come out in case he got hurt. Fortunately he was a great big man with a booming voice and he was able to talk them down a bit and they dispersed.

The younger girls were also affected by the popularity of drugs on college campuses. They adopted the habit of taking their own cans of drink to parties in case the communal punch had been laced with L.S.D.

The 1960s saw the breakdown of many traditional codes of dress and behaviour. This was true across the generations, and Betsy particularly welcomed the growing acceptance of trousers for women. She noticed, however, that changes did not occur everywhere at the same pace. When she moved to a small town in Pennsylvania in 1971, women attending university social functions were still expected to wear hats! It was among the young, however, that changes in behaviour were most marked. To Betsy it was as if a sharp dividing line could be run across the decade at about the beginning of 1967. The eldest daughter, who graduated in that year, "would not have dreamed of doing the things that the others a year later did so easily".

Betsy's single most overwhelming impression of the decade, however, was its aura of optimism:

There was so much hope and money going into research. Howard's job had been heading a research and development group for the I.E.E.E. (Institute of Electrical and Electronics Engineers) in New York. It caused him to run over to England a number of times. We went to Russia and Germany, and we went to the West Coast for a couple of conferences. And it was so easy to be mobile and find a new job. And it was an exciting time to put children through college. They were so full of hope that they could change the world. All of a sudden, at the end of the decade, the doors closed. There was a recession and there was a different attitude in the government towards research. Jobs were more difficult to find and that was the end of a fascinating era.

LuAnn Ganley: Growing up in Small-Town America

Born in 1950, LuAnn Ganley grew up in the very different atmosphere of a small town in Western Pennsylvania. The society of her childhood was predominantly white and

Protestant. Although the state of Pennsylvania had no segregation laws the small black community was ostracized to the extent that LuAnn hardly realized it was there.

You just did not mix socially. I did not have any black children in any of my school classes all through elementary school and Junior High (12 to 15 years). . . . Mostly they stayed up in Chevy Chase (the black area of town), went to church in Chevy Chase, had their social life there, and just did not come into the community. I think that at that time they probably would not have been accepted.

No hairdresser in the town would cut a black person's hair, and a local millionaire, who had built a swimming pool for the town children, swore that he would fill it in and plant flowers in it rather than allow a black person to bathe there.

Conventions in dress and behaviour were strongly enforced by local pressure. Women, for example, "did not wear slacks unless they were going on a picnic. They wore dresses. Even when she did the housework, my mother did not wear trousers; she wore a dress." Such a community was unlikely to accept the new wind of the Sixties with much enthusiasm, and LuAnn Ganley, who lived there all her life until she went to teach in New Jersey in 1981, absorbed many of the attitudes of small-town America. On the other hand, it was during the 1960s that she passed from childhood to

54 An American family sets out on a picnic in the late 1950s. Note the neat, almost formal clothes of the mother and daughter. Ten years later the same scene would probably have looked very different.

adulthood and began to question values that she had once automatically accepted. She was, therefore, more open than many in the community to new ideas. All these factors influenced her reactions to the 1960s.

One of LuAnn's earliest political memories is the 1960s presidential election. She saw Kennedy in person during one of his whistle-stop tours:

I remember going up-town and being put on my dad's shoulders and seeing this man who was very handsome standing up and talking to us. He had real long hair. Everyone else around had crew-cuts, even though if you look at pictures of Kennedy now, his hair seems short.

As a youngster LuAnn was swept along by the glamour of the Kennedy image, a tribute, perhaps, to the skill with which the President exploited the new medium of television:

You really identified with Kennedy — at least people my age did. It was like you were right there. You saw John Kennedy as a compassionate and strong father to his family and as a dynamic leader. And, of course, Jacqueline was the epitome of class, elegance and beauty. I remember watching her White House tour on T.V. It was magnificent. They actually took you through the White House. You just felt you were part of things.

Four months after her twelfth birthday, however, LuAnn was made aware for the first time of how small and insecure a place the world really was. During the tense days of the Cuban missile crisis:

I remember being terrified by the fear that we were going to be blown up. I remember the increase in air-raid drills in school, getting under your desk and pretending there was an atom bomb raining down on you. I read about it in the papers, and it was the first time I had become involved in something of an international nature. I was appalled that Cuba was so close and that the Russians in Cuba could actually hurt *me*.

The trauma of Kennedy's assassination added

to her feeling of insecurity, which was probably heightened by the fact that her own father had died the year before:

I was sitting in my American history class in the Junior High. I can even remember the room number. First of all there was an announcement that he had been shot and immediately all the teachers left us and we did not know where they had gone. And nobody talked, nobody did anything, and this was in a class with all kinds of kids, not just the good ones. Then came the announcement that Kennedy had been killed. I was shocked and stunned and tears started running down my face. I looked around and everybody in the class, from your roughest, toughest football player to your most sensitive girl, had tears streaming down their faces.

During LuAnn's years at the Junior High, the "Swinging Sixties" came to Western Pennsylvania. Local teenagers discovered the British pop culture; British rock music, Beatles' haircuts and even British accents became fashionable. Adults put up a strong resistance. Boys who turned up for school with fashionable hairstyles were sent home. When mini-skirts came in, teachers made all the girls

. . . kneel down, and they would measure how far your skirt was from the floor. At first your skirt had to touch the floor, then it had to come to the middle of your knee. And then as skirts got shorter and shorter, they would allow you two inches and then four. By the time I was in Senior High [1965 – 8], they had stopped doing it.

If young people soon won the battle to dress as they pleased, conventions among adults took longer to break down. In 1964 the wife of the new Presbyterian minister caused a scandal by appearing at the bank in shorts. It was not really until the 1970s that such things ceased to matter much.

LuAnn Ganley was never much concerned with civil rights issues. The local black population, very much in a minority, kept a low profile. Although in March 1965, 5000 people marched through the town in sympathy with the Selma marchers, LuAnn does not remember it. Among her family comments on the civil disobedience campaign in the South were generally unfavourable. The Vietnam War generated a lot more local heat. At first LuAnn accepted the official version of the war as an anti-Communist crusade that was for the good of the Vietnamese people themselves. Most of her relations felt the same way. Her uncles, who were members of the American Legion and the Veterans of Foreign Wars, made comments like: "We're there to protect the South Vietnamese people. We're there for the highest moral goals." There was much family criticism of draft-dodgers and demonstrating students.

Politically and personally, 1968 was a memorable year in LuAnn's life. Her mother died at the end of 1967 and the family was split up, LuAnn and her sister going to live with an aunt and uncle. That summer she graduated from high school and enrolled at the local university. At the same time she began to turn against the war. Her motives were personal and humanitarian rather than political:

The thing that really did me in was Bobby Kennedy coming out against the war and questioning what we were doing there. Since I had admired John Kennedy so much, that made me take a second look at Vietnam. I stopped thinking about the goals and started thinking about what was happening there. A very good friend of mine had a brother who had gone to Vietnam to serve as an officer. I remember him coming home and saying, "Hey, it's not all it's cracked up to be over there. My men didn't want to follow me into battle. There were men who shot their 2nd Lieutenants rather than follow them under fire." When you hear things like that from someone who was actually there, you begin to think that something is wrong. . . .

What got me upset was that there were people over there dying and no end in sight. I just wanted them home. I think that like most Americans, if the war could have been fought and won quickly, I would have been happy with that. . . . It just dragged on too long.

In 1968 such doubts were radical by local

55 A divided nation, 1968. Construction workers demonstrate on Broadway in favour of Nixon and the Vietnam War.

standards. There were many arguments at the family dinner table, with the generations being lined up on opposite sides.

On the other hand, LuAnn, by temperament and upbringing, was no revolutionary. In this she reflected the mood of her college as a whole, in which about 80 per cent of the students came from similar small-town communities. There were a number of anti-war rallies on the campus between 1968 and 1972 but attempts to organize boycotts of classes failed. The only disruptions that LuAnn can remember were those caused by heavy snowfalls and an epidemic of head-lice. She had little time for full-time campus militants:

I may have been a little cynical but I did wonder about the protestors' motives – if they were just trying to copy the larger schools [universities] or if they were really sincere.

Overall, she found the closing years of the decade rather depressing:

We were still in Vietnam and people were still dying. There were so many assassinations, starting with John Kennedy, then Malcolm X and Bobby Kennedy – that one really tore everyone up. And of course Martin Luther King had died a couple of months before Bobby Kennedy. So many horrible things were going on.

The one bright spot was the moon-landing:

It amazed me. I was glued to my T.V. set. When he said, "A small step for man, a giant step for mankind," I got goosebumps all over. It was something to be proud of. It made you feel so good when everything else was so bad.

Much of the passion and violence of the 1960s passed LuAnn's hometown by. Nevertheless, it did change. Some of the changes would probably have happened anyway, for the college expanded during the decade to become the largest state university in Pennsylvania and the population of the town became more diverse. Narrow ethnic and religious prejudices began to fade out. Other changes were a direct result of the 1960s. In the last years of the decade, the black population adopted a higher profile and picketing of the swimming pool began. It was finally desegregated in 1971. Rigid rules about dress began to disappear. When LuAnn returned to the Junior High as a teacher in 1973, staff were permitted to wear trousers and students could wear practically anything. The most striking change of all was the extent to which LuAnn's once hawkish uncles had lost faith in the rightness of America's mission abroad. By 1970 they were expressing a suspicion that the war was a mistake and that the troops ought to be brought home. Even today, when the war is discussed in the Ganley family, "My uncles will say: 'Well, I think we made a mistake.' And that is something I never thought I'd hear from them."

For LuAnn herself the impact of the decade was more personal:

If I had to pick one thing that shaped my character in that era it would be the assassinations. . . . It made me a much more insecure person. I don't want to say that I am afraid of the future but the assassinations, plus the fact that my parents died within six years of each other, made me aware of the brevity of life. If I wanted to achieve anything I had to do it now. If I had any goals I had to reach them by the time I was 40. Maybe every young person feels that way, but I'm sure that for me it was accentuated by the times I lived through.

Diane Grieves:
Growing up in North-East England

In 1960 Diane Grieves was 11 years old and had lived all her life in a working-class suburb of Newcastle, where her parents and grandparents had also grown up. It was a close-knit community, in which the power of unspoken conventions was very strong. Children were not encouraged to be ambitious or to envisage a life different from that of their parents. Although intelligent, Diane left school at 15 without any qualifications, and at the time she felt no resentment:

No one expected us to do "A" and "O" levels or go to college. I don't think I knew anyone who did . . . school just wasn't regarded as being particularly important. I don't remember anyone ever discussing with me what I might do when I was grown up, as I often do with my own children.

As elsewhere, there were many conventions concerning dress and day-to-day behaviour:

Even at the age of 11, you didn't wear trousers unless you were going to the beach. And you would never go to the shops with shorts on.

Class distinctions were clear-cut. Even in the same street, there was little contact between those who lived in rented houses, as Diane's parents did, and those who owned their own homes. During her early childhood, three doctors lived in private houses up the road and she would never have dreamed of playing with their children.

Although Diane's father, who worked in a local factory, earned enough money to keep his family "comfortable", the home environment was somewhat spartan. Their house had no piped hot water or indoor lavatory. Baths were taken in a tub in front of the fire or at a relative's house. Diane's mother always seemed busy and rarely had time to relax. For a long time the family's black and white television set was the only one in the street. On Sunday evenings their neighbours would gather in the living room to watch their favourite programmes.

Nevertheless, Diane's early childhood was happy and secure, until, at the age of 13, she began to rebel. In this she was quite different from her two sisters, who were 16 and 14 years older and had grown up in an earlier era. To a large extent they had absorbed the values of the community around them. Diane's rebellion started in the summer of 1962 when she was invited to her first grown-up party, given by the elder sister of a schoolfriend. She liked "the way people there dressed and the freedom of being able to talk about all sorts of things rather than just listening to adults

talk". After that, she and a friend began skipping school on Wednesday afternoons and going to one of the new discotheques which had opened in Newcastle. Suddenly, Diane discovered the exciting new youth culture, and the lives of the older people around seemed dreadfully dull and restricted:

I developed a set of expectations – things that I wanted – which weren't long-term things but things that I wanted to enjoy *now*. I didn't care what happened in five or ten years.

She met other young people with the same ideas, and from then onwards to be "one of the crowd" – "to belong" – became an important part of her life.

Fashions were crucial. Clothes were a public statement of who you were and to which group you belonged and distinguished you from adult society:

When I was about 14 there was a phase of very high-collared Victorian blouses, long skirts and

56 Beatles fans at a concert in Doncaster, December 1963.

very pale make-up. I wasn't allowed to wear things like that. They said I looked a "mess" and as if I was "walking the streets". So I used to get dressed secretly, pin up my skirt and put my coat on over the top as if I was going out quite normally, apart from my dead-pan white face. When I reached the corner, I would let my skirt down. But by the time I was 15 I wore my skirts very short and they went on getting shorter all the time.

Diane's parents took it all with a sense of humour, but her sisters were outraged. They called her a "hussy" and warned her ominously that she would attract the "wrong sort of boy". Pop music was an equally important part of the scene:

You lived to go out in the evenings to discos. A lot of people thought they were dens of iniquity with drugs and everything but really they were just fun places with loud music.

On one occasion Diane spent all night in a sleeping bag on a frozen pavement outside City Hall in Newcastle queuing for tickets for a Rolling Stones concert. She also went to see the Beatles when they came to the area, although "for me the Stones always came before the Beatles".

Among the young people of Newcastle the stimulant drug known as "purple hearts" seemed readily available, but few of Diane's close friends tried them. Neither did she have any contact with more potent drugs. For Diane "music was as intoxicating to my brain as drugs or alcohol. Even in the house, if a certain song was played, I would go into a world of my own, oblivious to everything else."

The youth culture broke down class barriers. No longer could you tell by a person's clothes or interests what social class he or she belonged to. The crucial distinction now was between those who were "with it" and those, young and old, who were not:

We all went to a place called the Go-Go in Newcastle, which was a discotheque with live bands. It was *the* place to go and you rubbed

57 Scooters – the status symbol of the 1960s' "mod" – on London's Carnaby Street.

shoulders with everybody. It didn't matter if they were doctors' sons or the rag-and-bone man's sons. These people all got invited to the same parties, and you'd be dancing with someone from one class at one moment and someone from another class the next. That was definitely something new.

Among Diane's crowd there was little interest in politics or in wider issues. The radical politics of the late 1960s, the turmoil in the universities at home and abroad, the crisis of conscience caused by the Vietnam War – all passed them by:

It comes back to this thing of living for today. . . . Most of us were concerned about nuclear arms, but as far as anything else was concerned it was too serious. We were more interested in jumping on the back of someone's scooter and going down to the coast.

Diane was exceptional in that she had her more thoughtful side. In 1962, at the time she was rebelling against the social conventions, she joined C.N.D. and took part in marches and demonstrations. In this she broke with the family tradition that politics were not the concern of women and that it was rather disreputable for young girls to march in public waving banners. The horrors of the Vietnam War, which were shown nightly on television, disturbed her, but there was no one with whom she could discuss her uneasiness:

My parents believed what they were told by the media. The American government must have a good reason for what it was doing and to criticize it was a bit odd. No one could see that you might have a point.

Everyone suddenly seemed to have plenty of money. In 1965 Diane began to train as a nurse. Her wages were low, and the only way that she could keep up with fashion trends was by relying on the generosity of her parents. They did not deny her much. When she asked for £5 (a lot of money in those days) to buy a penguin coat (a short, flared coat in shiny, brightly-coloured P.V.C.), she was given it, much to the horror of her sisters. In the neighbourhood,

Cars, which had been rare in our street, were now parked outside every other house. And television had become second nature. I particularly remember that tape-recorders — those big ones with the spools — became the thing to have.

In 1965 Diane's parents bought their own bungalow on a modern estate, something they had never been able to afford before. It had all the modern conveniences. There were plenty of jobs, even for the unskilled. When Diane gave up nursing in 1969 she never doubted that she would find a new job immediately — and she did.

The years between 11 and 21 are the years of transition from childhood to adulthood. Everyone changes. Diane believes, however, that the person she is today was at least partly shaped by the fact that she grew up in the 1960s. The atmosphere of the time encouraged her to reject her parents' values and begin a search for an identity of her own. While, in the short term she often slavishly followed the fads and fashions of her group, in the long term she developed into a more "critical and independent" person than she might otherwise have become. In this she compares herself to her sisters, who "are still living in the same area and doing and thinking the same sorts of things they have always done. . . . If I had not broken away, the pressures on me to be the same would have been very great."

DATE LIST

1960

February   Sit-ins by Blacks at Woolworth's lunch counter in Greensboro, North Carolina, begins an intensive phase of the non-violent struggle for civil rights in the U.S.A.

March   Sharpeville massacre.

June   Belgian Congo becomes independent and civil war begins.

September   *Lady Chatterley's Lover* trial.

November   Election of John F. Kennedy as president of U.S.A.
Sino-Soviet split becomes public.

1961

April   Yuri Gagarin becomes first man in space.

May   South Africa becomes a Republic and leaves the Commonwealth.

August   Building of Berlin Wall.

1962

July   Telstar I launched.

September   James Meredith enrols at Ole Miss.

October   Opening of Vatican II council.
Cuban missile crisis.
War between China and India.

1963

April   Beatles' first No. 1 hit, "From Me to You".

June   Assassination of Medgar Evers.
Profumo scandal in Britain.

August   Civil rights march on Washington.
Martin Luther King's "I have a Dream" speech.

November   Assassination of President Kennedy.

1964

June   Imprisonment for life of Nelson Mandela.

August   Gulf of Tonkin incident commits U.S.A. to all-out war in Vietnam.
First U.S. troops go into combat.

September   First disturbances at Berkeley.

October   Election of Labour government in Britain.
Downfall of Khrushchev.
First Chinese atom bomb exploded.

1965

February   Assassination of Malcolm X.

March   Operation Rolling Thunder begins bombing of North Vietnam.
Selma march.

August   Voting Rights Act passed in U.S.A.
Watts riots.

November   U.D.I. in Southern Rhodesia.

1966

February   Overthrow of Nkrumah of Ghana in a military coup.

June   Cultural Revolution begins in China.

1967

May   Secession of Ibos from Nigeria.
Civil war begins.

June   Six Day War in the Middle East.

August   Riots in Detroit and Newark.

December   First heart transplant operation.

1968

January   Serious student riots in Japan in protest at visit of U.S. nuclear-powered submarine.

February   Election of Dubcek as Czech party leader.

April   Assassination of Martin Luther King.
Riots in Washington come within two blocks of the White House.

May   Student revolt and general strike in France.

June   Assassination of Robert Kennedy.
French general election results in victory for de Gaulle.

August   Soviet invasion of Czechoslovakia.
Chicago Convention of Democratic Party.
Civil rights movement in Northern Ireland begins.

September   Musical *Hair* opens at Shaftesbury Theatre, London.

October   Mexico Olympics.
Great anti-Vietnam War protest rally in London.

November   Election of Richard Nixon as President of U.S.A.

1969

July   First men on the moon.

August   Woodstock rock festival.

1970

January   End of Nigerian civil war.

May   Demonstration at Kent State, Ohio.

June   Election of Conservative government in Britain.

BOOK LIST

As yet there are few balanced histories of the 1960s. The books listed below are of three types. Some are analyses of particular aspects of the 1960s, written by people who had strong feelings about why something happened and what its significance was. Most of them were written very close to the events in question and contain varying amounts of personal prejudice. The books in the second group relate personal experiences (rather like the biographies in this book), while the third section contains works, both fiction and non-fiction, that made an impact at the time, even though that impact was often short-lived.

None of these books presents anything like a complete picture of the 1960s, but any of them will help to capture something of the flavour of the time. Most of them are available through the British public library system.

Books about the 1960s

A. Aldridge, ed., *The Beatles Illustrated Lyrics I and II* (London, 1980)

C. Booker, *The Neophiliacs* (London, 1969)

R. Kennedy, *Thirteen Days: The Cuban Missile Crisis 1962* (London, 1969)

D. Kimche and D. Bawly, *Sandstorm: the Arab-Israeli War of 1967. Prelude and Aftermath* (London, 1968)

B. Levin, *Pendulum Years: Britain in the Sixties* (London, 1970)

R. Mabey, *The Pop Process* (London, 1969)

B. Masters, *The Swinging Sixties* (London, 1985)

C. Reich, *The Greening of America* (London, 1971)

Rolling Stone Illustrated History of Rock and Roll (London, 1981) (covers the late 1950s and the 1970s as well)

T. Wolfe, *The Electric Kool-Aid Acid Test* (London, 1969); and *Right Stuff* (London, 1979) (on two very different aspects of American life in the 1960s)

World Review: The Year in Pictures 1963–9

Personal Experiences

E. Amadi, *Sunset in Biafra: A Civil War Diary* (London, 1973)

V. Bukovsky, *To Build a Castle: My Life as a Dissenter* (London, 1978) (set in the Soviet Union of Khruschev and Brezhnev)

E. Burdon, *I Used to Be an Animal but I'm All Right Now* (London, 1986) (The experiences of a 1960s' pop star)

E. Cleaver, *Soul on Ice* (New York, 1967)

B. Fall, *Vietnam Witness* (London, 1966)

T. Hayden, *Trial* (London, 1971) (one of the Chicago Seven)

N. Hunter, *Shanghai Journey* (New York, 1969) (an American caught up in the Cultural Revolution)

Lennon Remembers: The Rolling Stone Interviews by Jann Wenner (Penguin, 1973)

Liang Hang, *Son of the Revolution* (London, 1983) (a Chinese teenager during the Cultural Revolution)

Malcolm X, *The Autobiography of Malcolm X* (1965)

P. Salinger, *With Kennedy* (New York, 1966)

Books that influenced the 1960s

J. Baldwin, *The Fire Next Time* (1963) (the black experience of the 1940s and 1950s that foretold the violence of the 1960s)

J. Braine, *Room at the Top* (1957) (one of the first of the British "working class" novels)

S. Carmichael and C. Hamilton, *Black Power* (1967)

B. Frieden, *The Feminine Mystique* (1963) (the first feminist tract)

R. Ingrams, ed., *The Life and Times of Private Eye 1961–71* (1971) (extracts from the influential satirical magazine)

Mao Tse-tung (Mao Zedong), *The Thoughts of Chairman Mao* (1966) (the "Little Red Book", Bible of the Cultural Revolution and cult book of Western student radicals)

M. McCarthy, *Hanoi* (1968) (the other side of the Vietnam War)

M. McLuhan, *The Medium is the Message* (1967) (the book that predicted the coming of the electronic technological revolution)

D. Storey, *This Sporting Life* (1960) (another novel of British working-class life)

Some Cult Films of the 1960s

Not necessarily the most popular or profitable films of the decade, but ones that could not have been made at any other time.

West Side Story (1961)

Saturday Night and Sunday Morning (1961)

How the West was Won (1962) (the first cinerama film)
Tom Jones (1963)
Dr No (1963) (the first of the James Bond movies)
The L-Shaped Room (1963)
This Sporting Life (1963)
Dr Strangelove or How I Learned to Stop Worrying and Love the Bomb (1964)
A Hard Day's Night (1964) (the first Beatles film)
War Game (1966) (banned by the BBC)

In the Heat of the Night (1967)
The Graduate (1967)
Hang 'Em High (1968) (the first of the Clint Eastwood westerns)
2001 – a Space Odyssey (1968)
Easy Rider (1969)
I am Curious Yellow (1969) (the first frankly pornographic film on general release)
If (1969)

BIOGRAPHICAL NOTES

58 Black Power spokesman, Stokeley Carmichael.

Carmichael, Stokeley. Militant black leader and advocate of Black Power.
Castro, Fidel. Born 1926. Nationalist revolutionary who became a Communist in 1961. Prime Minister of Cuba since 1959.
Cochrane, Eddie. Popular rock and roll artist of late 1950s. His biggest hit was "Summertime Blues". Killed in a car crash in 1960.
Cohn-Bendit, Daniel. Born 1945. "Danny the Red". Sociology student at the University of Nanterre, near Paris, whose expulsion sparked off the French student revolt of 1968 and who emerged as their most publicized leader.
Debray, Régis. Born 1942. French author of *Revolution in the Revolution? Armed Struggle and Political Struggle in Latin America*, which became popular among left-wing students. Died 1969.
De Gaulle, General Charles. Born 1890. President of France 1958–69. Died 1970.

59 French student leader, Daniel Cohn-Bendit, demonstrating outside the BBC TV Centre in London. On his right is British student leader, Tariq Ali.

Dubcek, Alexander. Born 1921. First Secretary of the Czech Communist Party February 1968 to April 1969. Led the liberalization of Czech life during the "Prague Spring".

Dutschke, Rudi. Leader of the Socialist Students League (S.D.S.) in West Germany, whose wounding in April 1968 triggered off the most violent weekend of rioting in that state's history.

Dylan, Bob. Born 1941. American song-writer and folk singer. Cult figure of the 1960s.

Gowon, Major-General Yakubu. Born 1934. President of the military government of Nigeria 1966–75.

Guevara, Dr Ernesto, "Che". Born 1928. Latin American revolutionary and guerilla fighter. Author of *The Guerilla War*, a handbook for revolutionaries in the Third World. Became something of a cult figure among the young, especially after his death at the hands of the Bolivian army in 1967.

Hayden, Tom. In 1960 he was a student at the University of Michigan and a civil rights worker. Disillusion with conventional politics led him to become a founder-member of the S.D.S. and author of *America in the New Era* (1963), which explained the disillusion of American youth with existing society.

Hendrix, Jimi. Born 1943. Dynamic singer and guitarist of the drug era. He made his name at the 1967 Monterey Festival when he burned his guitar on stage. Died 1970.

Johnson, Lyndon B. Born 1908. President of the United States 1963–8. Instigator of the Great Society anti-poverty programme and two civil rights bills. In 1964 he committed the United States to full-scale involvement in Vietnam. A controversial figure. Died 1973.

John XXIII, Pope. Pope 1958–63. Set up the second Vatican Council, which initiated important reforms in the Roman Catholic Church.

Kennedy, John F. Born 1917. President of the United States 1960–3. Assassinated on 22 November 1963 in Dallas, Texas.

Kennedy, Robert F. Born 1925. Brother of the President and Attorney-General 1961–4. A possible Democratic contender for the Presidency in 1968, he was shot in Los Angeles in June 1968.

Khruschev, Nikita. Born 1894. First Secretary of the Soviet Communist Party 1953–64. Died 1971.

King, Martin Luther. Born 1929. Black civil rights leader and advocate of non-violent methods to achieve social and legal equality with Whites. Assassinated by a white man, James Earl Ray, in 1968.

Malcolm X. Born 1925. A leader of the Black Muslims, who preached total separation of black and white society. Assassinated 1965.

Mao Tse-tung (Mao Zedong). Born 1893. Chairman of the Communist Party of China 1949–76. Instigator of the Cultural Revolution. Died 1976.

Marcuse, Herbert. Born 1898. Marxist philosopher of German birth, who had lived in the United States since 1945. During the 1960s he became the philosopher and spokesman of the radical student left. Died 1979.

Nixon, Richard M. Born 1913. Republican President of the United States 1968–74.

Nkrumah, Kwame. Born 1909. African nationalist leader and first Prime Minister (later President) of Ghana.

Ojukwu, Lieutenant-Colonel. Born 1933. Biafran leader 1967–70. Fled to the Ivory Coast at the end of the civil war.

Rubin, Jerry. One of the original Berkeley student rebels of 1964 and an organizer of the anti-Vietnam War protest movement. Later in the 1960s he became the high-profile leader of the "Yippies", a drop-out sect.

Smith, Ian. Born 1919. Leader of the Rhodesia Front Party and Prime Minister of Southern Rhodesia 1962–79, whose all-white government declared U.D.I. in 1965.

Stalin, Joseph. Born 1879. Soviet ruler 1924–53.

Wilson, Harold. Born 1916. Leader of the Labour Party 1963–76 and Prime Minister of Britain 1964–70.

60 The funeral of President Kennedy, 25 November 1963. On the left is the late President's brother Robert, who was himself assassinated in 1968.

INDEX